"This is truly an unforgettable and amazing story—heart-wrenching, inspiring, and ultimately reassuring. There's no denying the searing pain of heartbreak, but also no denying the strength of the human spirit to carry on. I can't imagine a person that this wonderful book won't touch. I loved reading every page."

—Wolf Blitzer, CNN anchor

"A work redolent with the wisdom and the joy wrung from pain. Eyal and his family deepen our understanding of what it means to love."

—Rabbi David J. Wolpe, Sinai Temple, Los Angeles,
and author of *David: The Divided Heart*

"Rabbi Charles Sherman's odyssey with his son, Eyal, who suffered a catastrophic brain stem stroke, is a masterful portrayal of a family with courage, fortitude, and eternal hope against all odds. The way Rabbi Sherman weaves his tale with personal stories, insights into Jewish tradition, undefended honesty about his own personal growth, and much more is a truly enriching read. Have a tissue (or a box of tissues) with you—because you will laugh, cry, and jump for joy at different parts of this remarkable book. It will open your heart and stretch your soul."

—Rabbi Dov Peretz Elkins, co-editor,
Chicken Soup for the Jewish Soul

"Charles Sherman's book on loss touches the heart. It validates the deep emotional price we all pay when faced with serious challenges. In the process, Rabbi Sherman softly helps the reader to turn loss into something positive; gently, ever so gently, one is able to learn from the hurt of the past while moving forward to a new day. He does all this with a sense of gentility, sensitivity, and an awareness of God's role in making all this possible. It is beautiful reading."

—Rabbi Avi Weiss, senior rabbi of the Hebrew Institute of Riverdale,
founder of Yeshivat Chovevei Torah and Yeshivat Maharat,
cofounder of the International Rabbinic Fellowship

THE
BROKEN
AND THE
WHOLE

Discovering Joy after Heartbreak

Lessons from a Life of Faith

∞

CHARLES S. SHERMAN

SCRIBNER

New York   London   Toronto   Sydney   New Delhi

SCRIBNER
A Division of Simon & Schuster, Inc.
1230 Avenue of the Americas
New York, NY 10020

First Scribner trade paperback edition March 2015

SCRIBNER and design are registered trademarks of The Gale Group, Inc.,
used under license by Simon & Schuster, Inc., the publisher of this work.

For information about special discounts for bulk purchases,
please contact Simon & Schuster Special Sales at 1-866-506-1949
or business@simonandschuster.com.

The Simon & Schuster Speakers Bureau can bring authors to your live event.
For more information or to book an event contact the Simon & Schuster Speakers
Bureau at 1-866-248-3049 or visit our website at www.simonspeakers.com.

Manufactured in the United States of America

1   3   5   7   9   10   8   6   4   2

Library of Congress Control Number: 2013037360

ISBN 978-1-4516-5616-9
ISBN 978-1-4516-5623-7 (pbk)
ISBN 978-1-4516-5624-4 (ebook)

For Leah

Always

What a precious find is an Eishet Hayil—

A Woman of Valor!

Her worth is far above rubies . . .

She looks to the future cheerfully.

She opens her mouth with wisdom;

Her tongue is guided by kindness . . .

Her children come forward and bless her,

Her husband praises her [and says]:

"Many women have done superbly, but you surpass them all."

Proverbs 31

Humpty Dumpty sat on a wall,
Humpty Dumpty had a great fall.
All the king's horses and all the king's men
Couldn't put Humpty together again

—ENGLISH NURSERY RHYME

Contents

Normal	1
Perseverance	17
Optimism	31
Faith	47
Anger	59
Regret	75
Time	85
Acts of Loving-kindness	95
Connection	109
Personhood	125
Communication	141
Marriage	159
Gratitude	171
Joy	185
Epilogue	197
From Eyal	203
Author's Note	207

THE
BROKEN
AND THE
WHOLE

Normal

∾

Late July 1985. I am stretched out on a chaise lounge at Elm Beach, a man-made lake in the Pocono Mountains. Greased with sunscreen, I'm immersed in a rabbinic text, one of many books I brought with me to prepare for my fall sermons, adult education classes, and other synagogue duties. Around me, dozens of kids play—with inner tubes, kickboards, shovels, pails, and sieves. The cacophony of laughter, yelling, and the occasional whistle interrupts my reading. My two daughters, eleven-year-old Nogah and nine-year-old Orah, both accomplished swimmers, engage in a competitive round of Marco Polo while Erez, our younger son, almost three, busies himself on the shore making mud pies. My wife, Leah, sits at the water's edge, chatting with friends and keeping an eye on things. Our other son, Eyal, four years old, plays nearby. He "swims" by flopping in two inches of water, rolling over several times, and giving his best impression of a beached whale.

A bell chimes, and soon we are serenaded with the theme song from the old movie *The Sting*. Three o' clock, right on time: the ice cream truck has arrived. I hum along as kids abandon the water and run to their parents, demanding money. They descend upon the truck like ants at a picnic. Eyal, our chubby toddler, with his straight strawberry-blond hair, a face like Buster Brown, terrific pinchable legs, and a tummy that hangs over the waistband of his red bathing trunks, leads the way.

He orders his Fudgsicle, gulps it down, and gets back in line. While other kids are still running to the truck, clamoring for firsts, he wolfs down his second serving and gets back in line yet again for thirds.

With Eyal, there is never any in-between. He is a child of extremes. He exhibits tremendous intensity and concentration, spending hours at the kitchen table working on a jigsaw puzzle of several hundred tiny pieces without getting discouraged. At these times he is precious and darling, but at other times the force of his emotions shocks us. His temper tantrums go far beyond anything we've experienced with our other kids. Five or six times a day, his body goes rigid and he emits a piercing howl while staring up at us and pulling at his ear. Nothing we do can end these episodes; they last until he drops to the floor and falls asleep, exhausted. But when he awakes from his sleep, he is instantly his precious self again—as if nothing has happened.

I watch Eyal move again up the line, thinking to myself, *This is one of the good moments.* Smiling, I consider how much I love my family, my life, and this place. Normal, everyday life, lived to its fullest. Simple, peaceful pleasures thoroughly enjoyed. Is there anything better? I believe it will last forever.

I can't remember a time when I didn't want to be a rabbi. I enjoy the rituals, the emphasis on family and community, and the intellectual challenges. Being Jewish feels natural to me, almost instinctive. I attended Jewish day schools and grew up in a home with a strong Jewish presence, from the kosher food my mother prepared to the Shabbat candlesticks, to the Kiddush cups, to the prayer books, to the Humashim (Bibles), to the Jewish newspapers. Judaism wasn't just a part of who I was; it was *everything*. Almost everyone in our neighborhood was Jewish. My father, an immigrant from Eastern Europe, made the synagogue community our extended family. It was always an honor to have the rabbi visit and enjoy a cup of tea or stay for dinner.

Very few people get to live their dreams. But there I was, forty-one years old, the rabbi of a major congregation in Syracuse, New York, and married to my summer camp sweetheart. As a preacher, I was passionate, creative, confident, energetic, and well-known in the greater community. I was on a career path that I believed would one day lead me to become rabbi of the largest, most prestigious synagogue in North America. I was also on my way toward building the large, warm, tight-knit family I had always imagined. My children were growing up with a strong sense of identity and appreciation for Jewish values, and they were turning out to be good kids who cared about one another and knew how to get along. I could imagine the day when each of them would graduate from college, fall in love, find meaningful work, and build a strong, cohesive family of his or her own.

Not that every last detail was perfect. I had more trouble than most balancing career and family. My job encompassed not merely the administrative side of running a synagogue of about one thousand families, but officiating at weddings, funerals, Bar/Bat Mitzvahs, and other life-cycle events; writing sermons; teaching adult education classes; overseeing a Hebrew school and youth programs; counseling people in distress; and participating in community events. I had to be ready to handle an emergency at a moment's notice, and I had to look the part of the serious, dignified rabbi at all times.

Except when I was at Elm Beach. There, nobody knew me as a rabbi. There, I could hang up my usual attire—dark suit, white shirt, sedate tie, wing-tipped shoes—and dress in a bathing suit and flip-flops. There, I could be my authentic self, joking around without worrying what others might think. There, I could forget about spiritual questions and focus all of my attention on what we would eat for lunch or what book I would read for pleasure after the kids went to bed. In an age before laptops and cell phones, Elm Beach was the closest thing I had to an escape, and I treasured it.

On his way back to the water, Eyal stops by my lounge chair, licking fudge from his fingers. Chocolate is smeared on his upper lip, chin, and cheeks. "Eyal," I ask, "did you bring me anything?" He hands me a clean stick and two nickels. "Thanks, buddy," I joke. Grasping the other two sticks, he darts off to Leah at the water's edge. Finding a small blue bucket, he plops down and begins to dig with his shovel and the sticks. Pretty soon, all of the kids have gathered around. Eyal and Erez dig vigorously, and a playful water fight has broken out between Nogah and Orah. My wife takes out tissues to wipe Eyal's face. She rubs more sunscreen on the kids and admonishes Nogah and Orah to stop splashing. Once again I reflect on what a wonderful, simple moment this is. Everything feels right. Everything is good. Everything is in its proper place. Smiling to myself, I return to my book.

• • •

We cannot always identify the precise point in time when our lives are transformed. For my family, it was 2 A.M. on a frigid March night, eight months after that trip to Elm Beach, when I awoke to a child's whimper.

"Leah," I said, "Eyal is crying."

"Yes, I know."

The last thing I wanted was to crawl out of bed. But Leah was six months pregnant with our youngest daughter, Nitza, and her physical state took precedence. I tiptoed to Eyal's room so as not to wake the other kids. His *Sesame Street* comforter was rolled into a ball, his pillow on the floor. Clearly he had not been able to find a comfortable position. I felt his forehead and found it very warm. Not good, but not a disaster, either. I would give him Tylenol and call our pediatrician in the morning.

"Eyal, let's go to the bathroom."

No response.

"Eyal, let me help you. You'll feel better." I reached into the bed, the old fireman's carry. "Here, let Abba carry you."

I carried him the few steps to the kids' bathroom, the "blue bathroom," as we called it, tiled in retro blue and cluttered with hair ribbons, cartoon-character toothbrushes, and bath toys. Easing him down the side of my body, I placed him before the toilet, maintaining a strong grip on the sides of his hips. Without my assistance, he would have crumpled to the floor. I attributed his fatigue to the late hour. Then I noticed his pasty color, his jiggling legs, his incoherent speech. His favorite yellow and red pajamas were drenched in body fluids, and his eyes were distant and unaware. At that moment, before I even called out to Leah for help, I knew: something was terribly wrong.

Over the next twenty-four hours, we went from pediatrician to radiologist, back to pediatrician, to pediatric surgeon, hospital admission, general pediatric unit, and finally, to the pediatric intensive care unit (PICU). At first, they said he had pneumonia, then congestive heart failure. They tapped and drained his chest cavity of several quarts of fluid and placed him on oxygen. They intubated him and put him on a ventilator to sustain his breathing. They restrained his hands to keep him from pulling out the tube in his mouth that stretched down his trachea. They ran test after test. Finally, this is what we were told: Eyal had a lesion the size of a golf ball intertwined in his brain stem, the part of the brain that controls basic human functions, breathing, and blood pressure.

"Take him home, enjoy whatever time you have left," they said. "If you're lucky, you'll have a year. More likely, just weeks."

It was devastating. As a rabbi, I often lent moral support to others when they received such news. Now I was the one being told to make the most of a short amount of time, and I didn't know what to do. The doctors had given up on Eyal. They didn't allow the slightest glimmer of hope. Somehow, we were supposed to do nothing about Eyal's condition— just sit back and watch him die. More difficult still, cruel even, we were supposed to "enjoy" these last moments.

Leah and I weren't ready to let Eyal go. There had to be an answer, we thought, treatments or procedures our local doctors didn't know about. We called anyone with the slightest knowledge of Eyal's condition. When one lead didn't pan out, we found other leads. The challenge occupied our minds and prevented us from becoming despondent. We felt that we were at least doing something; we had not yet exhausted all options. Given our fierce love for Eyal, we were prepared to do anything in our power—*anything*—to keep him alive.

We finally found a surgeon in New York City willing to operate on our son, well aware of the serious risks. Eyal came through the surgery, with most of the lesion removed. Our hope was restored. We were jubilant. Then, a few days after the surgery, he suffered a brain-stem stroke and slipped into a vegetative coma.

Four months passed. Leah and I stayed with Eyal, leaving our other kids with my parents back in Syracuse. We lived out of a suitcase in the hospital's parents' room, taking turns sleeping and sitting bedside. When Eyal woke up, he was intellectually intact. Mouthing his words, he told Leah and me his name, who we were, the names of his siblings, the numbers up to ten. He even smiled when I made a joke. Eyal was Eyal! Responsive, kind, funny. But his body was totally broken. He was quadriplegic, vent dependent. Our joy at being able to talk to him, at seeing him smile, was tempered by our fear and apprehension about his physical limitations.

We knew that his life—all of our lives—would be different. Only a handful of kids with Eyal's physical challenges had ever survived more than a few years. All the normal things I had expected to witness during Eyal's childhood— Eyal hopping on a school bus for his first day of kindergarten, learning how to play basketball in the driveway, learning to write his name—would never come to pass. He would always require intensive and expensive round-the-clock care; our lives would revolve around monitoring him and providing for his medical needs. Forget about casual family evenings out. Forget about family vacations. Summers at Elm Beach would be a thing of the past.

Six months after that horrible night with my feverish son in the blue bathroom, Eyal was transferred to a hospital in Syracuse about a mile and a half from our home. Eighteen months later, we moved him again, to a specially equipped room in our house. It had been just over 730 days and finally we were able to come home with our son. Leah and I made sure that someone in our family was with him twenty-four hours a day, no exceptions. My waking hours were divided between serving as rabbi and attending to Eyal's needs. Our privacy was invaded, with nurses and other caregivers coming and going throughout the day and night. We had accepted that this was the way it would be. We had no choice. At least he was alive.

Years passed. Eyal did not succumb, as we had been told he would, and our family managed to survive, even thrive, under the strain. Leah and I reclaimed a reassuring sense of home, not merely for Eyal but for all of us. Sure, there were countless hospital admissions, sometimes lasting months, but we always managed to bring him back and start again. When we had him at home, we did not sit around agonizing about all Eyal and our family couldn't do. Instead, drawing on internal reserves we didn't even know we had, we focused on making the most of what we *could* accomplish. We surprised ourselves. No, we couldn't live our lives exactly as we had been accustomed to, but we still experienced and sustained joy, love, and delight. We achieved a "new normal," not by putting the traumas behind us and moving on—that was impossible—but by discovering that we could live with what we had lost and, out of that, build something new.

This adaptation didn't happen all at once, and it didn't come easily. In my case, it required a comprehensive change in outlook—an intellectual, emotional, and spiritual shift that began that night in the blue bathroom. Prior to my son's illness, I could be self-centered and arrogant. I saw the world in black and white; it was either yes or no, right or wrong, kosher or *treif,* my way or no way. Afterward, I looked more honestly on my strengths and limitations and found myself more accepting, tolerant, generous, and forgiving. I came to distinguish between the essential and the irrelevant, and so began to live my sermons rather than just mouthing nice-sounding platitudes.

I learned to appreciate friendship and honest, authentic connections with others. I learned to embrace a broader definition of community, realizing that illness and vulnerability don't observe distinctions based on class, gender, race, national origin, and faith, and that random acts of kindness can come in the most surprising of places from the most surprising of people. I learned the value of real prayer and developed a richer, more meaningful relationship with the Divine. I came to open myself up across many dimensions of life, not perfectly, but enough to allow me to dream new dreams and feel happy and grateful for what is.

Today Eyal is thirty-two years old. He still lives with Leah and me at home. He is physically compromised, dependent upon others twenty-four hours a day for his most elementary physical needs. A ventilator breathes for him, while a feeding tube provides nutrition through a hole in his stomach. An ileostomy bag handles his waste; a vesicostomy, a small surface opening in his stomach, allows urine to flow freely; tarsorrhaphies, in which both his eyes are partially sewn shut, prevent corneal breakdowns.

Eyal cannot speak, walk, or move his limbs. The aggressive therapies given to him have left him with hearing loss, low blood counts, and kidney failure, among other problems, while his lack of mobility has made him vulnerable to bedsores, wound infections, and broken bones. We still cannot say how long he will live. A large chunk of the lesion remains in his brain; it appears to be inactive, but every six months he goes for a brain scan. Given how compromised his immune system is, the slightest illness—even a common cold—poses a dire threat. Just when we think nothing else can go wrong, wham, it does.

Despite all this, Eyal's mind still functions well, and in fact he sees himself as a "regular kind of guy." He recognizes that his health is fragile and that most people don't depend on all kinds of medical equipment for their daily survival. But because we have gone out of our way to include him in the life of our family and community, because we have treated him as "normal" and prodded others to treat him that way as well, he has come to think of himself as occupying his own proper place in the world.

It took him twelve years, but he graduated from Syracuse University with a degree in fine arts. He faithfully attends religious services at my synagogue and participates on the pulpit, albeit without speaking. Thanks to the Internet and a computer he controls with his chin, he keeps up with what's happening in the world. He makes some of his own decisions: what he wears, what he wants to do, who he wants to interact with. Although unable to talk, he still expresses his desires passionately. Not that we let him get away with anything. He teases us, and we tease him back. He is our Eyal. He has grown from the four-year-old, Fudgsicle-eating child at Elm Beach into a smart, artistic, thoughtful, compassionate thirty-two-year-old man. I am proud of him, proud that he is my son. I am proud of us for doing all we had to do, and continue to do, to help him become who he is today. And I am proud of all that I learned along the way.

I began writing this book of stories and reflections without knowing it in March 1986, the day of the blue bathroom. During many intense, anxious, nearly impossible nights spent awake in hospitals or sleeplessly pacing the hallways of our home, I scribbled on three-by-five cards, scraps of paper, even napkins. At first, the notes were practical in nature, items like questions for the doctors, lists of resources, and telephone numbers. Then I began to include random musings, details about people I had met and events I had witnessed, sayings that stuck with me over time. I did not admit it to myself, but there was another reason for keeping a written record of our experience: Writing allowed me a means of processing the incomprehensible. Writing allowed me to be both patient and therapist, to be parent and child, to be rabbi and congregant.

I may have had my notes in hand, but I wasn't ready to write a book about my family's experience. I wasn't ready even to talk about it. People in our community kept asking: How did we do it? How had our marriage survived? How had we maintained our faith? How had we prevented our other four kids from becoming mean, cynical, angry, messed up? Behind these lingered other, deeper questions: How had we resolved that awful contradiction between good and evil? Where had we gathered the strength and emotional resources to get up and greet the next day?

After some years had passed, I realized I needed to talk. The tragedy we faced, the shattering of our dreams and the peace we had known, was not just my family's story.

Everyone experiences difficult, life-altering circumstances at some point—the death of a loved one, illness, divorce, professional setbacks, economic failure. Some people are destroyed by tragedy and loss. They wallow in self-pity, their spark of life extinguished. Or sometimes people respond to difficulty and trauma with anger. They carry their heartbreak with them and go on to live painful, unhappy lives. But I can see now it is *because* of Eyal's unique circumstances that my family and I have come to affirm and celebrate life in a rich and meaningful way, beyond what I ever would have thought possible. I have discovered, much to my own surprise, that although we cannot wish or hope our losses away, we can thrive by changing how we think. We can dream new, more realistic dreams—and take greater satisfaction in attaining them. And maybe my insight and personal experience could help others who are fighting their own public and private battles.

Now, almost thirty years since Eyal first fell ill, I feel ready to share our journey. As I near retirement, I have come to understand exactly what it took to rebuild after our old life had been permanently destroyed. I see the mental and emotional challenges I encountered, the shifts I had to make, the work I still have to do. I am convinced that if I can honestly describe the elements of my personal and spiritual transformation to others, they, too, might be able to shift their own ways of thinking into helpful, healing ways.

Moses led the Israelites on a forty-year journey from slavery in Egypt to the Promised Land. When the Israelites arrived, they were physically exhausted and emotionally spent. They didn't know what the future held. All they knew was that they were following this guy Moses, who had introduced them to an unfamiliar concept of God. Having grown up in a culture of idols—objects you could see and touch—they had a hard time accepting Moses's notion of an intangible God, one nobody ever saw or heard. Their discomfort had become apparent earlier in the journey, when God summoned Moses up to Mount Sinai to receive the Ten Commandments inscribed on stone tablets. In Moses's absence, the Israelites became frightened and doubting. Believing that Moses would never return, they followed Egyptian practice and fashioned an idol to worship, a golden calf. They assumed that this tangible object would protect them in times of danger.

When Moses returned, he saw what his people had created and was consumed with anger. Under his leadership, the people had already been liberated from Egypt and led safely through the Red Sea by God's hand. If they still couldn't believe in the one true God, what more could Moses do? He cast the Ten Commandments to the ground, shattering them. Then, pulling himself back together, he turned around, went back up the mountain, and received a second set of tablets to replace the first.

These second tablets accompanied the Israelites on their remaining trek through the desert and became a focus for religious ritual and communal life. Biblical commentators have asked: what happened to the first set of broken tablets, the shards, the shattered pieces?

The text doesn't say, and the story is incomplete. But some scholars offer an interpretation that I like. They suggest that the shards were gathered and placed in the Ark of the Covenant alongside the second set of whole tablets—the broken and the whole together. The Israelites did not simply disregard their lack of faith. They attained a spiritual wholeness, but their imperfection always remained with them. It was by learning to live with their imperfection that they became healed and whole.

The Broken and the Whole explores the challenges we all face if we are to become content and fulfilled after sorrow and heartbreak: gathering the broken pieces and carrying them with us as we continue our journey to the Promised Land.

When I heard Eyal's terrible prognosis, my life was shattered. But eventually, as Moses did, I got up and climbed the mountain again. Slowly and sometimes painfully, I picked up the broken pieces of my life—dreams, ambitions, relationships—and carried them with me. Today, the brokenness is who I am, but so, too, is the intact, healed life I have been able to build.

Many people doubt that joy can exist after profound disappointment. When Leah and I are out with Eyal at the supermarket, the synagogue, or the mall, people give us pitying, sorrowful glances. I can almost hear them asking, *What kind of life can that family have?* On one level, they are right. Day to day, Leah and I are almost entirely absorbed in Eyal's complex physical needs, which is frustrating, scary, and exhausting. We have had to make enormous compromises.

But what people can't see are the deeper dimensions. The Promised Land isn't a place. It's in our hearts. There is an inner peace that comes from doing the best we can for someone we love. There is joy in witnessing someone with challenges stretch to accomplish ordinary tasks the rest of us take for granted. After so many years of caring for Eyal, we Shermans have fully committed ourselves to creating our own happiness. It is the intangibles that allow us to say, "Life is good."

• • •

Looking back on our journey, there was one moment when I knew we had made it. Ten years ago, we finally sold our vacation house at Elm Beach. I spent twenty years fixated on that little place in the Poconos. It represented a time when life was simpler, less complicated, less painful. Even as we parted with so many of our other dreams, I refused to give up Elm Beach. Every year, I paid the mortgage, taxes, utilities, and homeowner's fees, clinging to the notion that a miracle would happen and that we would one day return.

After twenty years of carrying this with me, I finally acknowledged that we would never go back. And with that sudden understanding came a more important realization: we already had. I was living Elm Beach each and every day, *re-creating its deeper meaning within my ordinary life.* I was experiencing joy, family, and a feeling of peace and satisfaction in my daily interactions with Eyal, in our family Sabbath dinners, in milestone occasions we were able to celebrate together, in my work as a rabbi. It wasn't Fudgsicles eaten on a hot summer day. It wasn't long afternoons whiled away in my bathing suit on a chaise lounge. It wasn't escaping my life. It was my life. And it was enough.

Perseverance

W hen we get sick, when we lose our house or our job, when we get divorced, when anything bad happens to overturn our lives, talk of finding renewed joy and contentment might seem hopelessly idealistic. Isn't surviving the day-to-day hard enough? How do we rise each morning and find the strength to handle both what has happened and the new challenges we must face, when what we really feel like doing is curling into a ball and huddling under our blankets?

Before Eyal got sick, I used to associate perseverance with notable people who defied the odds to accomplish great things. I thought of business executives who grew up in grinding poverty or athletes who overcame setbacks to become champions. I didn't think about the average Joe or Jane who just got up in the morning and did what needed to be done. Now, decades later, I understand that living itself can be a heroic act.

In May 2009, twenty-three years after we discovered the lesion in his brain stem, Eyal graduated from college, making us all incredibly proud. But what I remember most about Eyal's education isn't his being wheeled across the stage that day dressed in a black robe. Rather, it's a bitterly cold January day in 2003, similar to many others, when I watched him and Leah get ready to head to class.

It was the first week after winter break. Eyal had been taking courses for four years and had earned enough credits to rank as a sophomore. He had an 11 A.M. class called "Studio Art: Portrait Painting" that lasted for four hours (Eyal paints with a mouth stick). The weather was terrible, even by upstate New York's bleak standards. Bitter cold, wind chill of five below, icy roads, blowing snow. Many area school districts had either closed for the day or were delayed two hours to allow the plows time to clear the roads.

Our alarm clock went off at 5:45 A.M. Leah put on her robe and floppy slippers and walked downstairs to help.

"How was he last night?" Leah asked the night nurse.

"No problems." The nurse was already on her feet, holding a large syringe that pushed Eyal's morning medications and fluids through the gastrostomy tube, or G-tube, in his stomach.

Walking over to Eyal's bed, Leah found his eyes open; he had been waiting for her. She bent down and kissed his forehead, tickled his arms. "Good morning, Buttercup. It's a cold one! Snow day—but not for us." She opened the shades and turned Eyal's head toward the window, allowing him to glimpse the falling snow. Then she and the nurse worked together to reposition Eyal in his hospital bed.

First, Leah turned a crank, lowering his head. Working together on opposite sides of his body, they moved him by lifting the bed pad underneath him. The nurse took a large plastic feeding bag and filled it with several cans of a carefully measured nutritional supplement and Pedialyte. She and Leah examined Eyal head to toe to make sure that no

skin breakdowns or other problems had developed overnight. They gave Eyal his sponge bath and washed his hair
while he remained in bed. The nurse emptied his ileostomy
bag, containing his bodily waste. Using a Q-tip soaked in
rubbing alcohol, she cleaned his trache tube and put clean
gauze pads underneath the trache site.

With these tasks out of the way, Leah inserted Eyal's
hearing aids and artificial teeth. She gave him the first of his
many daily eye-drop treatments, since his brain stem does
not function well enough to tell his eyes to blink automatically. Next, the nurse pounded on Eyal's chest for about a half
hour to loosen whatever mucus had accumulated in his lungs
overnight. She gave him his breathing treatments through a
nebulizer and suctioned him out, using a large gray machine
called a coughilator that creates an artificial cough to bring
up phlegm. She performed a careful check of his vent, making sure it was working properly.

Leah walked over to the large, colorful "quote of the day"
calendar hanging on the wall. "Eyal, today is Thursday, January 24. The saying of the day is a Swedish proverb—'Those
who wish to sing always find a song.' Oh, and Syracuse University beat Seton Hall last night."

As the work continued downstairs, I went back to sleep
for another hour. At seven fifteen, I walked downstairs and
peeked into Eyal's bedroom. "Good morning, everybody. I'm
going to synagogue now. I'll be back after morning services."

I returned at around eight thirty to find Eyal already
dressed. Leah had gone to the closet to pick out his clothes,
large gray flannel sweatpants—the easiest to dress him in—a
short-sleeved, bright red Phillies T-shirt, and a thick wool
navy sweater, a hand-me-down from me. As always, Eyal
had disagreed with her selection. "I don't want to wear that,"

he had mouthed to Leah and the nurse. "I want to wear my SU blue sweatshirt and new jeans." Leah had gone back to the closet and found the right clothes. Over so many other things in his life, Eyal gets no choice. What he wears is something he gets to choose.

With Eyal now watching the *Today* show, the nurse took a well-deserved break and Leah went upstairs to get dressed. At nine fifteen, Leah came back down to position Eyal's Hoyer lift, a large metal hoist that uses hydraulic power to transfer him from his bed to wheelchair and back. The Hoyer lift also functions as a scale. Leah and the nurse placed him in the oversized nylon mesh sling and weighed him. Because of all the antibiotics Eyal has taken, his kidneys no longer function normally. He is always in renal failure, and he has a tendency to retain fluid. Because of his ileostomy, we must also meticulously track his weight in addition to his "ins and outs." Finally, by about a quarter to ten, Leah and the nurse were ready to transfer Eyal from the Hoyer lift to the wheelchair.

In order for Eyal to sit up properly, both the Hoyer lift and wheelchair need to be lined up precisely. If he is positioned incorrectly in the wheelchair, which happens frequently, two people have to stand on either side of him, holding him by the sides of his pants, and yank him up higher. Since Eyal has no head control, Leah has a little tool kit and uses the wrench to reposition his headrest.

Eyal controls his wheelchair with a chin switch, but he can only make gross motor movements, not the subtle movements necessary to navigate the narrow halls and angles of our house. He can drive around a large playground pretty well, but inside his driving is horrendous, as evidenced by the numerous gashes in our walls. On this day, as on most others, Leah stood behind him with a switch that allowed her to correct the unexpected bumps in Eyal's driving performance.

Leah and the nurse then dressed Eyal in his outdoor clothes—a parka and a warm scarf wrapped about his mouth and neck. They put mittens on his hands and an orange SU fleece cap over his ears, and put on his goggles to protect his eyes. They then covered him with two heavy blankets from chin to foot. Leah wheeled the chair down the ramp in our garage, while I got into the driver's seat, warmed up the red and white conversion van, and lowered the lift. As the nurse took her place in the back on the bench, Leah maneuvered the wheelchair into the van, where it was locked into place. The garage door opened and we were off to school.

The university is at most a ten-minute drive, but on this day, with the icy roads, it took us forty-five minutes. I pulled into a designated parking space, still about a hundred yards or so from the classroom building. Dozens of kids were walking into the building, most looking like they'd just rolled out of bed, many of them carrying coffee.

We repeated in reverse what we had done in our driveway. The lift worked agonizingly slowly. For a few moments, as he was being lowered, Eyal sat on the lift platform in the cold, with the wind blowing at him, quickly covering him with snow.

Leah eased the chair off the lift, Eyal's school backpack slung over one shoulder, a second backpack with his suction machine and other medical equipment slung over the other. Leah also carried a small shovel to clear a path to get to the building, while the nurse carried a Plexiglas book stand on a three-foot pole that attached to his wheelchair. She also brought a blue Ambu bag with which she could "bag"

Eyal—artificially inflate his lungs—in the event the ventilator malfunctioned. I rolled down the window and yelled
out to them, "Eyal, have a good day. Leah, I'll be at the synagogue, call me if you need anything. What time should I
pick you up?"

There was nothing unusual or special about this day. It
was very much like hundreds, even thousands, of other morn-
ings at our house. Except for the family, caregivers, and a few
close friends, no one knows how much work is involved in
getting Eyal up and going. Just dealing with the day-to-day is
extremely challenging. Over time, though, we've found ways
to keep ourselves afloat, even when we most want to give up.
These techniques for persevering paved the way for our long
journey back to joy and contentment.

My family is not alone in the effort it takes to get through
the day. I often sit with a family during a difficult time in
their lives to write a eulogy. The deceased may be an accoun-
tant, a homemaker, a small-business owner, a receptionist at
a doctor's office, a schoolteacher. I sometimes think I know
him or her well enough, but when I speak with the grieving family, I'm often told stories about the person and the
enormous challenges he or she has overcome. Spouses killed
in car accidents. Children fallen victim to drug or alcohol
abuse. Family members suffering quietly from debilitating
illnesses. How amazing, I think, that people can confront so
much and still manage to live ordinary lives. They go about
their business, undertaking a million little acts of defiance,
restating over and over again to the world that they won't let
life destroy them.

Looking at such people from the outside in, we say, "I

couldn't do that. I couldn't live with that." But with everything I've been through with Eyal, I've come to see that these folks don't regard themselves as heroes. They'd be embarrassed if someone expressed admiration for them. And maybe that's why they're able to do it. As incredible as it seems, living with adversity becomes part of who they are. The struggles they live with every day are no different from having red hair or blue eyes—they're just a part of their identities.

If someone had told Leah and me that we would have to spend decades of our lives caring for our oldest son, we would have denied we could do it. We would have protested that we didn't have the resources, the personality, the training, the temperament, the time, the patience. But we did do it. And we continue to do it. None of us understands the strength we have until we come face-to-face with the unimaginable. Only then do we discover that we do indeed have what it takes not merely to survive, but to live meaningfully, with intelligence, wisdom, confidence, and sometimes even with a sense of humor.

Our greatest teachers in all of this are often those most directly affected by hardship. Many years ago, we set Eyal up with a small percussion keyboard—a virtual drum set—that he could play with a mouth stick. Our family is musical and all our kids play different instruments, so we wanted Eyal to be able to participate. With his drum set, he was providing the beat for the Sherman family band. I see that as a metaphor for Eyal and his own perseverance. He does not want to be left out. He finds a way to join in, and the rest of us are better for it. His rhythm is not perfect, but his objective is just to live and stay active, one beat at a time. And because he keeps himself going, he helps the rest of us persevere as well. Every day that Eyal gets up is a day that we can put our fatigue, frustration, or gloominess aside and rejoice with him.

Perseverance has rhythms of its own. It is not a singular, isolated moment. There is no playbook. We tread on day after day, and before we know it, we've accomplished something. Eyal's younger brother, Erez, used to take piano lessons. One day, Leah drove Erez to his lesson in our large conversion van. A boy in Eyal's sixth-grade class was playing outside and waved at Leah. "Is Eyal taking piano lessons?" he asked. Our family still smiles at this. The only thing Eyal can move is his head, about one inch from side to side. I guess this boy was so accustomed to seeing Eyal take part in school activities—the school chorus, although Eyal had no voice; gym classes, although he cannot move; art classes, using a paintbrush in his mouth; the school band, playing a triangle with his mouth stick—that he just figured Eyal was taking piano lessons. Why not? Eyal was doing everything else.

In gathering strength to persevere, we can read about other people's experiences and their responses and feel encouraged, but for the most part, we have to make it up as we go along. We make mistakes along the way, but we tread on, day in and day out. One powerful approach, I've found, is to focus like a laser on what needs to be done *right now*, deliberately pushing aside any thoughts about the future or the past. If it's not germane to your immediate needs, stop thinking about it. Such focus requires discipline and regular practice, but it works. I know from experience that if I let myself think about the broader picture—what has happened, what could happen—I wind up feeling overwhelmed and depressed. Such emotions impede me from completing what I have to do just to make it through the day. So I deliberately put blinders on and ignore the larger picture. I accomplish tasks one at a time. Over the years, I've gotten better and better at this, so that now it happens automatically. Small drops fill a bucket.

In Jewish tradition, worshippers place prayer shawls over their heads at various points in the service, building a little tent for themselves. It looks strange, but it helps remove distractions so that you can dive deeper into prayer. Catholics concentrate on each prayer of the rosary, a single bead at a time, so that external concerns and anxieties fall away. Deep meditation in the Buddhist tradition is the same thing—a way to prevent unproductive thoughts from impeding your present purpose. Getting by in the face of disaster involves focusing on the task at hand, and then the next task, and the task after that. It really is that simple.

It also helps to surround ourselves with people who can support us emotionally. Our family doesn't just rely on Eyal's nurses, caregivers, therapists, and teachers to help satisfy his physical needs; we draw strength from them, and they draw strength from us. I have an old friend, Seymour, a fellow rabbi, who is also always there for me when I need him. I can call him any time of the day or night to seek out his advice and cry on his shoulder. He allows me to vent, he is not judgmental, and he makes me laugh.

In 1986, on the eve of Eyal's first surgery, I called Seymour, and hearing the anguish in my voice, he said, "Hold on, I'm coming there right now." Seymour lives in Philadelphia and presides over a large congregation. It was not easy for him to break away. But he came anyway, and the next morning the two of us found a private space in a conference room to pray. It meant so much to me not to be alone and to have the benefit of his wisdom.

A professor of Eyal's put it nicely. Asked during a media interview about what it was like to have someone like Eyal in her class, she talked about Leah and all the work she did to help Eyal get by each day, saying, "We all need someone in the room with us." We all need a shoulder to cry on, a hand to hold. As strong as we might be, as disciplined as we might become, we can't do it alone.

Jewish ritual emphasizes both the internal strength people need to persevere as well as the supportive role of relationships. Each week, Jews read publicly a small portion of the Five Books of Moses. It takes a full year at this pace to cover all five books, from Genesis to Deuteronomy. Every time a synagogue completes one of the Five Books, a communal response resounds through the sanctuary—"*Hazak Hazak V'nitchazak.*" Which means, "Be strong, be strong, and together we will be strengthened."

Why do we repeat the edict to stay strong twice, saying, "*Hazak Hazak*"? I think the repetition underlines the perseverance required to plod along and overcome life's challenges and bruises. We must remind ourselves frequently; you can't get by just thinking of it once. Those of us who have been tested—and that's all of us—understand that you have to double down on strength. You need physical energy and stamina, but more than that, you need mental staying power and emotional fortitude. "Together we will be strengthened" is a powerful reminder that we can't do it alone. Strength comes from the support of others and the support we can lend others.

In 2000, Eyal was medevaced to the Children's Hospital of Philadelphia (CHOP). He was dying of a blood infection and was wrapped in many blankets, almost like he was in a cocoon. When we arrived, the nurses removed the blankets, and I signed the necessary paperwork and said thank you and good-bye to the air ambulance paramedics. I heard Leah suddenly gasp and begin sobbing. It was so unlike her. I rushed to her side, asking, "Leah, what's wrong?"

"Eyal's teeth."

He had ground them down into his gums, apparently because he was in such pain. He can't yell, he can't groan, and we had not been able to see the agony on his face because he was so wrapped up in blankets. I began to cry, too. The critical-care doctor turned to us. He put his arm around Leah. "Don't worry. We're managing his pain now and will get him dentures. It will be fine."

The doctor did not understand why we were crying. It wasn't about teeth. It was about everything. We had worked so hard. All we had wanted was to create some kind of quality of life for our son. Now we found ourselves in yet another emergency situation, headed to yet another stupid hospital. We were uprooted and exhausted. The teeth felt like the last straw. We were overwhelmed.

Still crying, Leah and I looked at one another. We couldn't give up. We knew we had come too far. The next day, we felt better and more able to cope. Eyal recovered. And we had him fitted for dentures.

Perhaps the greatest realization I have had about perseverance is simply the need for all of us to believe in our own strength. We must never doubt what we can endure. Blind faith in our ability to persevere can itself become a kind of perseverance.

In late September 1987, Eyal was six years old. He had spent nineteen months in three hospitals, and we were planning to take him home. It was unheard of for someone with his critical needs to live outside of a hospital, but several new laws had been passed, which ushered in a new cultural attitude. Now society recognized that kids like Eyal should be in their homes rather than cooped up in institutions. With the increased availability of skilled home care, we were eager to give it a try. We thought it would be good for Eyal, for us, and for the other kids.

We wound up modifying our five-bedroom, white-shingled Cape Cod house to accommodate Eyal's needs. We built several ramps and relocated my study from the main floor to the basement, giving Eyal an easily accessible bedroom. We interviewed nurses for the necessary twenty-four-hour nursing shifts. We contracted with home health care providers and arranged for a backup ventilator. We ordered hospital linens, hospital gowns, medications, tubing, sterile water, canisters of oxygen, and cases of Pedialyte. We arranged for doctors to be on call. Lacking medical training or experience, Leah and I learned Eyal's complex care plan, in case a nurse failed to show. In effect, we were setting up a virtual pediatric ICU in our home.

All this frightened me, even as I rejoiced at the prospect of having Eyal home. While I had not always been happy with the hospital's abundance of arbitrary rules and requirements, at least the environment was familiar. Whenever Eyal experienced even the slightest problem, I just walked down the hall, hailed a passing resident or nurse, and hollered, "Help!" In bringing Eyal home, we would be sacrificing our peace of mind, not to mention our sense of privacy. We would have so many people coming and going at all hours: nurses, therapists, and people delivering medical supplies, oxygen, and hospital linens. It would feel awkward to discipline the other kids in the presence of people we hardly knew, or to engage in the usual husband-wife bickering.

The day before we brought Eyal home, as I was mulling all this over, I had a conversation I'll never forget. It took place in the public men's bathroom, steps away from Eyal's room at Syracuse's Crouse Irving Memorial Hospital. Standing before the sink was a tall man, a bit unkempt, with a five-o'clock shadow. I had never spoken to him before, but I had watched him for six weeks through the window between our hospital rooms. Every morning, he arrived at the hospital wearing dark green pants and steel-reinforced shoes. He sat for hours in a rocking chair, his little boy Michael snuggled in his arms and tethered to a ventilator. When Michael slept, his father caught a few winks. When Michael awoke, his father attended to him. Each evening, before leaving to work the night shift at a local grocery warehouse, the father turned down the lights, placed his son in his crib, bent over, and kissed him atop his head.

"How's your boy doing?" the man asked me through the men's-room mirror.

I told him we were taking Eyal home the next day and were worried, tired, and burned out.

The man gave me a compassionate look. In a measured tone he said, "Mike is my youngest. He has an older brother, Teddy, who's five years old. They are the spitting image of one another. A couple of weeks ago, Teddy began his first day of kindergarten. He took the school bus. What made it special is that Teddy and Mike have the same genetic condition. Teddy, too, is on a vent. You should have seen the kid—his first day of school. He was so excited, smiling ear to ear. He

29

went with his aide on a special school bus. We expect to have Mike home soon, too."

He walked to the paper towel dispenser, yanked down a towel, and dried his hands. "Good luck," he said. He reached into a shirt pocket, pulled out a pen, and scratched on an old receipt. "Here's my number."

I took the number and headed back to Eyal's room. Shaking my head, I said to myself, *I thought we had problems. This guy has two kids like Eyal.* But before I reached Eyal's room, the man caught up to me. He put a hand on my shoulder. "Hey, listen, don't feel sorry for me, please don't. That's life. It could be a lot worse. My boys are alive. One is home on a vent; Mike will be home someday soon."

I searched his eyes. There were so many things I wanted to discuss with him, so many things I wanted to know. "Can I ask you a question?" I said to him. "With everything else happening in your life, how do you do it? How do you persevere?" All these years later, his answer continues to resonate.

"You just do what you have to do."

Optimism

∞

October 25, 1986, our sixteenth wedding anniversary, didn't seem at all special. Eyal had been in a coma at New York University Medical Center for almost three months, utterly unresponsive and with no improvement. The doctors told us he would never wake up. If by some small chance he did, he would require institutional care for as long as he lived. There was no hope. None. Zero. Nevertheless, we spent the day of our anniversary at the hospital, where the great challenge was passing the time.

Hour after hour we sat, almost forgetting it was our anniversary. I was amazed how difficult it was to do nothing. The only activity was waiting for the doctor to make rounds, in the early morning and early evening. I read every available newspaper and made frequent treks to the candy machine. When I needed to stretch my legs, I counted the 347 square, beige tiles that lined the floor from the elevator to the men's room. I took note of the three water-stained ceiling panels that needed replacement in the parents' room. I approached the bulletin boards and reread what had been posted there: letters of thanks from parents, birth announcements from nurses, memoranda from hospital administrators, newspaper clippings of interest to the nursing staff, and signs saying things like "Do Not Park in the Visitors' Parking Lot." Leah sat at Eyal's bedside, often resting her head on the bedrail. She worked on the *New York Times* crossword puzzle and engaged in small talk with some of the nurses. Other times, she stared out the window at the East River.

That night, we had dinner in the hospital cafeteria, a large, soulless place that served bad institutional food. Long white tables and cheap chairs with blue vinyl covers filled much of the space; in one corner, a special seating area was reserved for doctors. The food servers all wore the same uniform, dark blue shirts, pants, and the required hairnets. Everyone eating in a hospital cafeteria looks exhausted and drained. We were no exception, even if it was our anniversary.

To mark the occasion, I had tried to lighten the mood by taking a cab some twenty blocks to one of our favorite restaurants, the Second Avenue Deli. I brought Leah's favorite meal: rare roast beef with Russian dressing on rye, coleslaw, and a Dr. Brown's cream soda. For myself, I ordered fatty pastrami on rye with lots of deli mustard, a hot dog with mustard and sauerkraut, french fries, and a Dr. Brown's black cherry soda.

As I walked in carrying our food, I found Leah sitting at a table. It was late for dinner, seven thirty or so, but people still lingered, mostly hospital employees, and I noticed some sideways glances at our feast. I gave Leah a Hallmark card from the hospital gift shop, the sole anniversary card hidden amongst all of the "get well" cards. Leah was pleasantly surprised, knowing I am not a big card giver. She reached over, squeezed my hand, and apologized for not having a card for me. We took a short mazel tov phone call from our kids and parents at the nurse's station.

A couple of miles away, at Shea Stadium in Queens, the Mets were playing game six of the 1986 World Series against the Red Sox. Coming back upstairs after dinner, I clicked on the television that hung in the corner of Eyal's cubicle to watch the game. Leah, not much of a baseball fan, humored me. She sat on the other side of the bed and read a book. A few innings into the game, she stood up, gently pinched Eyal's chubby cheeks, adjusted his blanket, and kissed his forehead. "I'm going to bed. Happy anniversary, Chuckles."

"Leah, you're blocking my view of the game," I said, teasing her. I stood up and gave her a hug. "Love you."

We were prepared to sit at Eyal's bedside for as long as it would take. Even though we had been told Eyal would never wake up, we felt differently. We would not allow the naysayers to strip us of possibility. It had nothing to do with science or scans. We were not prepared to jump ship on our son. We insisted he be given every opportunity to heal. Some may have accused us of being in denial, but that was fine. We didn't care what anyone called it. We were determined to stay optimistic.

I continued watching the ball game, doing play-by-play narration for Eyal, who remained someplace out there. Our son was a big baseball fan, and before his illness, he had loved to play. On Saturday afternoons in the backyard, he was everybody's favorite when we chose up teams. Although he was just a toddler, his physical size and menacing power were reminiscent of the Big Bambino, Babe Ruth. Eyal hit the ball well, although his base running left something to be desired. We did not know then that his fatigue, his heavy breathing and grunting, and his inability to round the bases were all a consequence of his lesion.

That night, Eyal had no idea if there was a ball game, who I was, who he was, and where we were, but I did the play-by-play because that's what I had always done with him at home. "Eyal, Darryl Strawberry is coming up to bat, a lefty. He bends down, takes some dirt in his hands, rubs them together, bangs on the plate three times, stares at the pitcher. He's ready; the pitcher winds up. Strawberry fouls the first pitch back over the first-base dugout."

I continued like this for several more innings before stopping, turning up the volume on the television, and just watching the game. Mookie Wilson stepped up to the plate for the Mets. I looked over at Eyal. His eyes seemed focused on the television. He squinted, tightened his eyes, and moved his mouth. It looked like he was mouthing the name Mookie. I considered the possibility. Of course not. It couldn't be. Wishful thinking.

The mind plays all kinds of tricks when we're sleep deprived. At times, I had felt convinced I had seen Eyal move his arm or leg. When it happened, I would rush to find a nurse. Inevitably, she would look at me sadly and say, "It's just an involuntary reflex, Rabbi Sherman. I'm sorry."

But that night, something seemed different. I kept watching my son.

A few innings later, Howard Johnson, the Mets' third baseman, came up to bat. Eyal's best friend in nursery school was a little kid named Howard Johnson. They did everything together. When Eyal came home from school, he told us, "Howard Johnson brought a little red dump truck for show-and-tell. Howard brought a cheese sandwich for lunch. Howard has a little brother, Charles."

Eyal squinted, and his lips pronounced the name "Howard Johnson." This time I was certain. I jumped up to get the chief neurosurgery resident. He was sitting at a desk at the nurse's station, jotting notes on a chart. "Duncan," I said, "quick, you've got to come over here."

Duncan was a preppy young man with thick, reddish blond hair and tortoiseshell glasses. He enjoyed visiting us and often helped Leah with the *New York Times* crossword puzzle. She would leave it on Eyal's tray table with a pen, and a couple of times a day when making his rounds, Duncan would look over the puzzle and fill in a few answers, even when Leah was not there.

Duncan rushed over to the head of Eyal's bed. He, too, saw what I had reported. Eyal clearly mouthed the words "Howard Johnson." I ran down the hall to wake Leah. Duncan dashed off to the OR to inform the attending surgeon, who was operating on a late-night emergency. "The Sherman kid is a Mets fan!" Duncan cried.

Leah and I didn't go to sleep that night. We wanted to make sure Eyal was really awake, that this hadn't been a figment of our imagination. And it wasn't. Day after day, a few moments here, a few moments there, Eyal came back. The doctors were encouraged but cautious. They were not sure what functions Eyal would regain. The ensuing weeks were once again a vigil, but a different kind of vigil, with Eyal talking to us, mouthing his words. We kept reassuring him, saying, "Everything is going to be fine." I sometimes wondered whether the words were intended more for us than for our son.

After several weeks, Eyal saw no further recovery. He never got off the vent. He was paralyzed from the neck down. But remarkably, his intellectual capacity was intact. We never got into long conversations with him about what had happened. If he asked, we would tell him, "You got sick, but you are getting better." And he never asked for more detail. It didn't seem to matter what had happened. This is where we were now. There was an innocence about Eyal. In trying to protect him, we were protecting ourselves. Instead of talking about what had been, we talked about what would be. "Eyal, when we get home, we're going to go to a baseball game," we'd tell him. Or, "We're going to go to Sylvan Beach. Everybody's waiting for you."

We had used so much of our energy and resources the previous few months, pouring them into our hope that Eyal would emerge from the coma. Now that he had awoken, we faced a new reality. What next? We realized Eyal would take our lead. We had no choice but to convey to him an attitude of optimism, even though it was nearly impossible to find that sense of hope within our own hearts and minds. I decided that the only thing we could do was just set small goals. We had to imagine a new and different future. We would meet each new goal one at a time until that new vision became a reality. And we did it. Again and again and again.

The Babylonian Exile, which took place around 586 BCE, was difficult for the Jews. They had been kicked out of their homeland in what is now the State of Israel and were forced to march to what is now Iraq. The Babylonians inflicted this displacement hoping to break the Jews' spirit, and by all accounts they succeeded. The Jews had seen their families dispersed, their holy city of Jerusalem destroyed, and their central place of worship, the Temple, burned. They were convinced that they would never return to the Promised Land to rebuild their city and repopulate their country.

Zechariah, a prophet who lived during this tumultuous time, preached a message of optimism. Claiming that the Jews would return to their homeland, Zechariah used a strange turn of phrase to describe the Jews—"*assirei tikvah*," literally translated as "prisoners of hope." Rather than meaning "prisoners," though, "*assirei*" usually connotes something tied up with rope or bound to something else. According to Zechariah, the Jews were bound with hope; it was part and parcel of who they were as a people. It is an essential part of who all of us are today, too. Hope isn't something out there for us to discover, it's something that's already tied to us, that's inside us. What we need to do—and never stop doing—is release it, express it.

Walking around hospitals, we saw people expressing hope all the time, every chance they got. One woman I met, Rochelle, had a teenage son who had been in a coma for more than a year. One day, in the course of conversation, she told me that one of her kids played tight end for his high school football team and was being recruited by several major college football programs. "Has he decided yet where he'll attend?" I asked.

"Oh, not yet, we're waiting for him to recover."

From the way Rochelle had been talking, I had assumed the football player in her family was a different child than the one whose hospital bed she sat beside each day. But that's the way people in hospitals talked about their kids: they didn't use the past tense; they always spoke in the present, their words keeping their hope alive.

• • •

As a rabbi, I try to release hope whenever I meet people struggling with extreme hardship. In March 2012, I went to see Marilyn, a woman in her late sixties. She had retired after forty years working as a clerk for the county, and her husband had passed away a couple of years earlier. Marilyn was overweight, had diabetes, couldn't walk, and was living in a rehabilitation center. She had fallen into a depression, convinced that she was never going to go home again. She never left her room, not even at mealtime. When I visited her, she was teary eyed. "I want to die," she said.

Before Eyal got sick, I would have taken her words at face value and spoken to her about death. I would have said something like, "Marilyn, life is a gift; we have to use each day the best we can. Life comes with pain and challenges." But this time my response was different. I felt I understood what she was really saying to me. She didn't actually want to die. She was saying that she felt she no longer had anything to hope for. Now I understand that the loss of hope feels like a sort of death. If hope is an essential part of who we are as human beings, living without it is like not living at all. Marilyn only needed to hear something quite simple from me. "You are going to come home again. I don't know when, and it may require accommodations and additional help, but you will be home again."

I said this to Marilyn, and it gave her hope. She has not yet gone home, but her mind-set has changed. She is working hard in her therapies. She is more social, she takes her meals with other residents, she talks more, she smiles more, she laughs more. No, we can't control everything that happens, but we can reconnect with our internal capacity to hope. When we think of ourselves as "prisoners of hope," life gets better, more tolerable. We become more accepting and carry the broken pieces of our past with us more easily. We open ourselves up to new possibilities in the present.

Eyal returned home after almost two years in hospitals, but he still spent all of his time either in bed or sitting in his wheelchair in our small family room, watching television. After a few months of this, one of his nurses, a young woman not long out of school, had an idea: "Let's take Eyal for a ride in the car."

We reacted with disbelief. Our car was a huge 1987 Chevy station wagon with wood paneling on the sides. To take Eyal for a ride, we would have to physically pick him up from his wheelchair, place him in the station wagon's rear area, prop him up with lots of blankets and pillows, and transfer his ventilator, oxygen tank, and suction machine to the backseat. We had never done it. We had never even considered it.

"Hey, want to go for a ride?" I asked Eyal.

He didn't answer.

"All the kids want to go for a ride with you," Leah added.

Before he could answer, we had sprung into action and were setting up the car. It was a group effort. When we had transferred all the equipment, the nurse, Leah, the kids, and I lifted Eyal from his wheelchair to the car. The rest of us got in, and off we went. The ride lasted at most fifteen minutes. We drove around the neighborhood, pointing out once-familiar sites—the school playground, the synagogue, the supermarket, the toy store.

A fifteen-minute car ride might seem insignificant, but to us it was a statement about possibility. Two weeks later, we reserved a medical transport van and rode a half mile with our entire family to a local shopping mall. All we did was sit together in front of the ice cream parlor and watch people walk by for an hour. But it was something. And like this we built upon our successes. We asked ourselves: if we could go for a ride like any other family, what else might we be able to do? We found a sense of hope, and this optimistic attitude itself created a kind of momentum.

Optimism became an imperative for our family. It was the only way we were going to survive. And if we were disciplined enough about staying positive, perhaps we could not just survive but thrive. Perhaps we could inspire others to grow with us as well.

In June 1993, Eyal graduated from elementary school and prepared to enter middle school in a new building. Considering his enormous physical challenges, Leah and I thought it best to meet with his seventh-grade teachers and introduce them to Eyal. We could appreciate how overwhelming teachers might find it to have a kid like Eyal in the classroom. They would hear beeps and alarms from the machines and need to know about necessary medical procedures like tube feedings. They would need to know how to reposition Eyal in his wheelchair, making sure his "pishy jar," a plastic urine-collection device, fit snugly so as not to create any embarrassing moments. They would need to understand his involuntary muscle spasms and his method of mouthing words. They would need to accept his entourage of Leah, a nurse, and a teacher's aide. Despite the challenge, we hoped Eyal's teachers would make him feel welcome. It would have been easy for teachers to ignore his presence, doing little things like not engaging him in the lesson, not waiting for his answers. We were asking for more effort and certainly more patience.

Several days before fall classes began, we sat with Eyal's team of eight teachers in a small administrative conference room. We shared our expectations and suggestions, listened to their concerns, and tried to answer their questions. We concluded the meeting with an unpretentious, genuine request: "Please dream with us."

About a week later, I received a letter from the woman who would teach Eyal seventh-grade math. I had met her for the first time at our conference. She was young, maybe in her midthirties. Her words brought home to me how an individual's optimism affects others. She wrote:

> *Dear Rabbi Sherman,*
>
> *I just wanted to thank you for taking the time to meet with Team 1 and help us understand Eyal's needs. On a personal note, I wanted to thank you for asking us to dream with you. I, as have most human beings, have spent many hours of my life asking the proverbial "Why?" and trying to find the courage to ask instead, "Why not?" It can be most difficult—sometimes seemingly impossible—to maintain a global perspective with respect to one's personal trials in life. It is often much more expedient to play the role of the beleaguered skeptic. Your request leaves me with both a sense of awe and a feeling of humility; if you can allow yourselves to dream, then I find I can do no less than dream with you. Thanks for the lesson.*

Hope is contagious. When we express a positive attitude in the face of suffering, a similar optimism fires up in others. Their lives become brighter, and they start to dream, too. A powerful upward spiral comes into being, enabling things to happen over time that nobody would have thought possible. Little by little, we heal and grow together. Some of our dreams come to pass, and we learn to part with those that don't. Life for all of us gets better.

The Bible offers many affirmations of optimism, including an important cautionary tale. The Israelites were on the doorstep of the Promised Land after fleeing Egypt. They were wary and concerned, not sure what awaited them in this new place. All they knew was that God had proclaimed His intention to deliver them from Egypt and bring them to a "good and spacious land, a land flowing with milk and honey." The Israelites insisted that Moses send twelve spies, one representative from each of their twelve tribes, to investigate the Promised Land. After several days, the spies returned. Ten of them were in total agreement: The place was terrific, even better than they had hoped for. It *was* the Promised Land. There were watermelons the size of boulders, grapevines so big it took two men to lift them. A great future in a lush, fertile land awaited them.

I can imagine how their words were greeted: with smiles, pats on the back, and rousing cheers. The Israelites' journey had been worth it. But then the same ten spies sadly reported something else that deflated everyone's spirits: The inhabitants of the land were giants. There was no way the Israelites would overcome them.

As the crowd's excitement dissipated, smiles became frowns. The people cried out in anguish and fear, questioning why they had left Egypt in the first place. Then the last two spies, Caleb and Joshua, jumped up onto a rock and announced, "It's true, as our friends said. It is the Promised Land. And it's true the land is delicious and lush, beyond our wildest dreams. It awaits us. And it is also true that there are giants who live in that place. But we will overcome these challenges. We will enter the Promised Land and succeed."

Caleb and Joshua were saying, "Don't give up on the dream." Confronted with this message, I imagine the Israelites felt conflicted. They heard similarities in the two reports, but the difference between the conclusions was stark. According to the story, God recognized that this generation of Israelites who had experienced Egyptian slavery wasn't ready to go into the Promised Land. Thanks to their enslavement, they had come to see themselves as small and weak. God realized that many more challenges lay ahead. And He probably said to Himself, *They don't have the stamina, the stubbornness, or the ability to dream and to hope. I can't build a people out of what I have here. You can't enter the Promised Land unless you believe in the promise.* And so the only two people from that whole generation who made it to the Promised Land were Caleb and Joshua. It was their belief in God's promise that made the dream a reality.

All of us have a Promised Land. And challenges and obstacles—the "giants"—always loom, preventing our entrance. But we are called to be like Caleb and Joshua, optimistic and confident in our ability to believe in the promise. Yes, dreams and hopes by nature are just that, dreams and hopes. Very few of us actually get to live happily ever after. But just because some of our dreams and hopes may appear dashed, we must never give up hoping and dreaming.

An ancient teacher, Rabbi Tarfon, said, "You are not obliged to finish the task, neither are you free to neglect it." The task is the dream. Nobody gets to finish all their earthly tasks, to realize all their dreams. Yet it's imperative that we dream big dreams, dreams that may seem unachievable, even though we will experience failure and disappointment. The task at hand—the dream—gives us a reason to live hopefully. Failure isn't *not* achieving your dream; it's the despair of not engaging the dream, not keeping it alive.

Never, ever deny a possibility. Never say a person can't do something. Instead, repeat to yourself, over and over again: hopes and dreams have a value of their own.

Orah, Eyal's immediate older sister, turned sixteen on December 3, 1992, when Eyal was eleven. "Today's the big day," she said to me first thing that morning. I picked her up after school and brought her down to the motor vehicle office to get her learner's permit. We were home from the DMV a mere ten minutes when she asked me to let her drive around the block. Eyal was living at home with us; he had a large blue wheelchair with an insert customized to fit his body shape, so as to prevent skin breakdown. We often wheeled that chair so that Eyal could sit in the kitchen before our large bay window. That day, Orah's birthday, he sat and watched her slowly drive around the block and pull into the driveway, with me in the passenger seat. When we came back inside the house, Orah was excited, while I was just relieved to be out of the car.

I came up to Eyal and rubbed his head. "Eyal, what did you think of Orah's driving?"

He didn't answer my question. "When I am sixteen," he mouthed, "can Dave make me a switch so I can drive, too?" Dave, the "switchman," was the guy from a local organization for developmentally challenged youngsters who designed and built the assistive technology Eyal used—computer switches that he could activate with his chin, a Plexiglas stand to hold his schoolbooks, simple toys he could manipulate by moving his cheeks or his eyes. Dave also maintained and repaired Eyal's wheelchair.

I didn't say, "I'm sorry, you will never drive." We have never told Eyal what he cannot do. I just smiled and said, "We'll see."

On May 3, 1997, Eyal turned sixteen. Among other gifts, I gave him a bright red toy Corvette with a remote control and said, "Eyal, this is the car I'm going to buy you someday." I was making a promise for us both, giving us a joint dream. Who can predict what somebody is going to create in the years to come?

Faith

Setting small goals and remembering that hope already resides within us can help us to sustain an optimistic outlook, but for me, optimism always has been rooted in something deeper: an unshakable sense of faith. I have stayed positive because even in my darkest moments I continued to believe in God. But people often ask me, "How do you regain faith after a devastating calamity like Eyal's?" I tell them I didn't *regain* my faith after Eyal got sick—I never lost it! When they ask how that could be, wondering what the secret to remaining faithful is when your world has been destroyed, my answer is that I honestly don't know. Somehow, one way or another, I have always believed. To this day, I continue to believe.

Faith that endures even amidst terrible suffering is not unique to me. Walk around hospitals, and you're sure to see it. One night in the NYU PICU, in the immediate aftermath of Eyal's stroke, I noticed that across the room, the grandmother of a six-year-old Dominican boy with encephalitis sat with hands folded, eyes closed, and lips moving in prayer. On a nearby nightstand rested a Koran belonging to the father of an Egyptian boy who had just undergone facial reconstructive surgery. A third child in the ward was being cared for by his parents, devout Jehovah's Witnesses. They had traveled across the country to this hospital so that their son's surgery could be done without a blood transfusion, which is forbidden by their religion. And in the bed adjacent to Eyal lay Squeaky, a fourteen-year-old girl from Bedford-Stuyvesant who had come for a heart-lung transplant. "I am not going to die," she exclaimed to nobody in particular. "Jesus is not ready for me yet!"

Rose Kennedy, the celebrated matriarch of the Kennedy family, lived through many trials and tribulations, including the death of three sons and a daughter, yet she made an effort to attend mass every single morning, even in cold, wintry Boston weather. "The most important element in human life is faith," she once wrote. "If God were to take away all His blessings: health, physical fitness, wealth, intelligence and leave me with but one gift, I would ask for faith. For with faith in Him and His Goodness, mercy and love for me, and belief in everlasting life, I believe I could suffer the loss of my other gifts and still be happy."*

And then there is the Biblical figure of Job, whose life raises the quintessential question of why tragedies befall seemingly honest, good people. Job is initially healthy, prosperous, married to a woman he loves, and the father of ten great kids. Nothing bad has ever happened to him. Satan comes along and taunts God, telling Him that the only reason Job is good and faithful is that he has never been tested. Take away his blessings, Satan says to God, humble him, and you will then discover the real Job, a man bereft of faith and belief.

*Rose Fitzgerald Kennedy, *Times to Remember* (Doubleday, 1995).

Following this conversation, Job's blessings are taken from him one by one. He loses his wealth, his home is destroyed, his children are killed, his body is racked with painful boils. "What have you done to have God punish you so?" his friends ask. His wife tells him to cast off his belief in God, but Job's faith remains strong. Defying all reason, he continues to bless God, saying, "The Lord has given, the Lord has taken away. Blessed be the name of the Lord."

In the end, Job is rewarded for his faith, restored to his former good fortune. It's easy to believe in God when things are good, and much harder when terrible things happen. Yet somehow, defying all logic and understanding, people like Job and Rose Kennedy and Squeaky and myself continue to believe.

I realize that "I don't know" is not a very satisfying answer. But perhaps it is more satisfying than it appears at first glance. Could it be that the persistence of faith hinges on our very ability to feel comfortable *not knowing*—that the more we can incorporate mystery and contradiction into our concept of God, the more we can believe even amidst our pain?

In the summer of 1997, when Eyal was sixteen, Leah and I accompanied him to Wilmington, Delaware, for surgery to correct scoliosis, a debilitating curvature of the spine, which in Eyal's case was the result of years spent sitting in a wheelchair. The surgery succeeded, but during recovery Eyal fell victim to a staph infection he picked up in the hospital. An anticipated ten-day hospital stay stretched to weeks and then months. I slept at the nearby Ronald McDonald House, a few minutes' walk from the hospital, while Leah slept at Eyal's bedside, as she always did when he was in the hospital. During the day, I sat bedside, allowing Leah to go back to the Ronald McDonald House to freshen up. We were like mother bird and father bird, taking turns on the nest, feeding and protecting our hatchling.

One night, after the lights had been dimmed and the very sick kids in Eyal's unit had been put to bed, I met a woman named Judy in the lounge outside Eyal's room. When she found out that I was a rabbi, she told me that her son Andy, a boy about Eyal's age, had been in a terrible car accident. No drugs, alcohol, or speeding had been involved. It had been raining and a car traveling in the opposite direction had lost control, jumped the median, and entered their lane. The car missed them, but the car Andy was in hit a utility pole. Three of the four kids walked away unscathed, not a scratch. Andy, who was sitting in the backseat behind the front passenger, got whacked in the head by the pole as it plowed through the car. Now he was blind, could not remember what he'd had for breakfast, slept all the time, and would probably require twenty-four-hour-a-day care for the rest of his life.

Judy turned to me, her newfound rabbi, and said, "Tell me, why should I believe in God? What good is God, if He let this happen? What did my Andrew ever do to anyone to deserve this?"

Her question flustered me. Since Eyal had taken sick, I had intentionally avoided asking questions like this. Just as we have to discipline ourselves to focus on tasks immediately before us in order to persevere, so sometimes we have to *will* ourselves to believe in God, refusing to let ourselves ask tough questions until such time as we can emotionally and intellectually handle it. It's not the most honest approach, but who cares about honesty when our survival hangs in the balance? I was terrified that if I began to seek answers, I would lose control of my own internal discourse and become bitter—a person who wanted nothing to do with the world and nothing to do with God. My faith, unquestioned as it was, was working for me, allowing me to affirm the present moment and feel grateful for what I *did* have—the ability to get up each morning and see my son. I couldn't bear the thought of breaking with my faith and losing my ability to cope.

By the time I met Judy, though, avoiding the tough questions was becoming harder. And Judy's inquiry, anguish, and frustration, her impatience for an answer, would not permit my indifference or silence. So here is what I said: "Judy, life can be hard. We all suffer sometimes. We get sick or a loved one gets sick. Life can be very painful and what makes it particularly difficult is that we often don't know why bad things are happening. It is very easy to blame God, but I believe that God is part of the solution to our distress and that He is always with us. God gives us strength to get through the hard times. God helps us see the joy and beauty of life—to be able to laugh and dance and celebrate, even if our hearts have been broken, and they *will* be broken. If you embrace God, you will find comfort. You will find a sense of peace despite your pain."

These words were not my own. I had been taught them years earlier as a means of offering comfort and understanding and now I turned to them without worrying about whether I actually believed them. Looking back on it, I am not sure they made Judy feel any better. I think just having a conversation with a "person of faith" allowed her to vent her frustrations and express her fear. That release probably did her more good than my answer itself.

• • •

It took me years to get to a point where I could articulate a different answer, one that reflects my own heartfelt philosophy. There were no real epiphany moments in those years. Instead I just tried to continually examine my own experience and study Jewish texts. I also became progressively more comfortable communicating to people what I really believed. Traditionally, rabbis didn't do that; they stuck pretty close to Jewish wisdom and didn't offer personalized sermons. But over the last ten to fifteen years, more rabbis have come to share openly their own personal stories, beliefs, and gut feelings. Although I still worry that conveying everything I feel will overwhelm my congregants, I've come to see how they yearn for honest and authentic musings about faith. I've also realized that I feel most moved and inspired when someone offers me his true beliefs and shares his personal stories. So that is what I've started trying to offer others.

Pop theology suggests that we see God in our ability to get out of bed each morning, even when every impulse we have tells us to pull the blankets over our heads and call it quits. God, we are told, is in the voice of a neighbor who calls every morning to check on you. God is found in that friend who offers to pick your kid up from school and handle the carpool when you are unavailable. Sounds great, but I don't accept that. Such a notion of God is too pat. It suggests that faith and belief are latent in all of the good in life, but that God has no role in any of its negative experiences. If you believe God is only good, yet at the same time all-powerful, how do you explain evil and senseless tragedies? You are left with an all-powerful God, an all-good God, who just allows these things to happen. You have to change the formula: either God is all-powerful but not all good, or God is all good but not all-powerful.

I am not ready to give up the idea of a God who is both omnipotent *and* all good. I have arrived at a notion of God that accounts for both the bad and the good. It runs like this: I admit I don't understand God. I never will. But I resolve to have faith in God's ultimate goodness anyway. Mystery and incomprehension are built *into* my concept of God, and in this way, God, like us, carries the broken and the whole together.

If I could go back and have that conversation with Judy again, I would tell her that I don't have a perfect answer to her question. Even in this day and age, when just about everything seems to be at our fingertips, there are certain things we simply cannot wholly understand. This reality makes us uncomfortable and uneasy, yet it's also the essence of faith. Faith is a willingness to believe in someone and something, even though parts of that belief appear incomplete or inexplicable. It's a willingness to admit that we don't know everything, and to feel to our depths that this is okay—that we can handle the mystery. Such faith is not neat and tidy, but it's the best we have.

I would also quote for Judy a verse from the Book of Deuteronomy, one that plays an important part in the Jewish liturgy of Yom Kippur, the Day of Atonement and Reconciliation: "The secret things belong to the Lord, but the things that are revealed belong to us and our children forever, that we may do all the words of Torah." We humans want to know everything. That's why we build towers of Babel and eat forbidden apples in the Garden of Eden. But as this verse suggests, we simply cannot know everything. There are "secret things." With each passing year, we gain greater knowledge of our physical world, but we will never really understand the kind of love, compassion, or selflessness that leads someone to forgive another or to run into a burning building to rescue a stranger. There are certain matters of the soul that will always defy mathematical or scientific explanation. We can't know if there's a heaven or if God exists. We can't know why bad things happen to good people. Humble acceptance of the limitations of our knowledge is where faith begins. Faith is learning to live in that zone of discomfort. Faith is learning to feel at home there. But faith is also action. It is an act of faith to take what we can know and use it to fulfill God's purpose on earth.

It's tempting and understandable to say, "Why me? What did I do to deserve this? It's not fair. Life is a bitch. It shouldn't be this way." Yet such sentiments reveal more about us than they do about God. When we say something is not fair or we do not deserve it, we haven't sat down with a scale and put our merits on one side and our demerits on the other side to see that our merits outweigh our demerits. No, what we really mean is: "I do not *want* life this way. I want it to be the way I want it." The thing is, life comes as it comes. It is what it is. Faith is our trust in our ability to handle that which we cannot control.

Moses's first conversation with God takes place on a mountain, at a burning bush. God instructs Moses to return to Egypt and inform Pharaoh that slavery is over and the Israelites' redemption is about to begin. Moses is not a simple shepherd; as a onetime prince raised in the court of Pharaoh, he is a scholarly, intelligent man. Before he takes on this enormous task, with all of its risks and dangers, he makes what appears to be a reasonable request of God: "Tell me, who are you?"

The question contains an element of disbelief. God

counters it with a strange answer, which Moses accepts without reservation: "I AM WHO I AM."

What does this mean? For many years, I puzzled over it. How could "I AM WHO I AM" have made Moses feel more confident? I now think I understand. God's answer was not ultimately about God. It was about life itself—a proclamation of life's inherent mystery and of our need as humans to accept it. Moses was looking for assurances and guarantees, but God was being honest and saying, "Uh-uh, it doesn't work like that. There are no easy answers." Just as God is who God is, so Moses needed to be who he was, realizing his potential and capacity to transform himself, his community, and the rest of the world. "I AM WHO I AM" suggests that engagement or conversation with God is fundamentally about seeing the world and ourselves honestly, and proceeding from there. "Moses, it is what it is. Now go out and do the best that you can, under the circumstances. You'll find that your best will be good enough."

When I imagine the conversation I wish I had had with Judy, and in my many ongoing conversations with myself, I try to remind myself that everything is what it is. There are certain things about God and life that I don't understand and never will, but I accept that. Sometime in the future I may gain further insight, but maybe not. Either way, it's okay. And truly believing that it will be okay, despite what I may or may not know—that is an expression of faith.

I admit that my faith is irrational—the way falling in love with your life partner is, or the way you know by feel that you have a soul. Faith is also an understanding that the punctuation of life is a question mark.

• • •

In 1986, when Eyal had that devastating brain-stem stroke, I did not retreat into myself. Maybe it's my personality or the pastoral aspect of my professional calling, but while we spent weeks at the hospital, trading shifts and waiting twenty-four hours a day for some kind of response from Eyal, I found myself mayor of the floor, acting as a resource for parents and caregivers. That's how I met Elchanan and his father. "*Elchanan*" is Hebrew for "God is gracious." Like Eyal, Elchanan was five years old at the time. He had traces of facial hair, a bloated stomach, and a swollen and puffy face, all the side effects of steroids given to reduce the swelling in his brain from an inoperable lesion.

Elchanan was born in King David's backyard, the Beth Israel neighborhood of Jerusalem. Both his mother, Chana, and father, Eliyahu, were blind, and so they had been unaware of Elchanan's distress for years. They hadn't caught the warning signs: a clumsy gait, the drooping of his mouth, increased drooling, his eyes fluttering and becoming unfocused. Elchanan had been brought to NYU by an association of selfless and generous women whose mission was to rescue kids in need of specialized medical care. Chana had remained at home in Jerusalem, caring for Elchanan's four siblings. Only Eliyahu had accompanied him on the journey to New York.

Eliyahu strolled the hospital corridors humming *niggunim*, hallowed hymns. A deeply devout, holy man, he never walked with his head uncovered, and he concealed his blindness by wearing large, dark sunglasses. His only obvious vice: he smoked like a chimney. His English was almost nonexistent. Knowing Hebrew, I sometimes served as a facilitator between him and the hospital staff.

Early one Friday morning, Eliyahu seemed particularly

ill at ease. The Sabbath was coming and friends had invited him to spend that evening and the following day with them in Brooklyn, a considerable distance from the hospital. He had not left Elchanan's bedside since their arrival several weeks earlier, and he was anxious. As mayor of the floor, I didn't hesitate. "Go. It's only twenty-four hours. I'll be around. I'll look in on him frequently. He'll be fine. You need the time. Have a good Shabbes."

Late Friday night, as promised, I called on Elchanan and found him resting comfortably. But it was not Elchanan who commanded my attention—it was his bedclothes and a banner that had been placed in the room. Every hospital has its own linen color scheme to better identify its laundry; here it was soft pastel blues. Elchanan was wearing his hospital-issued blue gown, but propped atop his head was a home-made pastel blue yarmulke, or skullcap. Someone from the hospital community, in an effort to create some semblance of comfort and familiarity, had taken one of those anonymous gowns and gone at it with scissors, needle, and thread. Someone had used the hospital computer to print a piece of Jewish theology on a large placard, then attached it to the wall facing Elchanan's bed. The paper stretched from window to door and contained a cardinal principle of my belief system: "I believe in absolute faith, in the coming of the Messiah, *even though* he may be delayed . . . I believe."

What stands out for me, all these years later, isn't mention of the Messiah but those two words, "even though." Some may consider these nothing more than a disclaimer undermining true belief. But they are the opposite. To me these words mean: "I am frustrated, I am angry, I am confused, I am looking for an answer, a resolution. This is not what I wanted in my life. But, *even though* I am hurting and impatient, I wait. I will hold on to faith and hope. I am convinced things will get better."

We all are tested. People of faith know there will be an "even though," and somehow, some way, we can still maintain a belief in the goodness of the world and in God. Every day when Leah or I walk into our synagogue, pushing Eyal's wheelchair up to his place in the pews, our presence and participation affirms those words on Elchanan's banner.

I believe. *Even though*, I still believe.

Anger

◈

One gorgeous spring day in April 1987, a little more than a year after Eyal had been diagnosed and while he was still being cared for in a Syracuse hospital, my two daughters kept him company while Leah watched our baby, Nitza, and I popped out to run some errands. It was a wonderful break. In upstate New York, after a long, brutal winter, the first clear, sunny days with a hint of warmth burst with rebirth and renewal. People smile; they're out walking their dogs, cleaning up their yards. I felt invigorated just going to get a haircut and stopping off at my office and house for a few minutes.

An hour or so later, when I walked back into Eyal's hospital room, I was unhappy to find the air unbearably stale, hot, and steamy. Someone had neglected to inform Environmental Services that springtime had arrived and it was time to turn off the heat. I wanted to open the window and let just a little spring in, but I couldn't. Eyal had MRSA, methicillin-resistant *Staphylococcus aureus*, a bacterial infection resistant to normal antibiotics. Its victims are usually long-term patients with compromised immune systems. If not contained, MRSA can infect an entire hospital and literally shut it down. Hospital guidelines require that MRSA carriers be placed in isolation, that their trash be double-bagged, that their laundry be clearly marked and washed separately. Those who enter an MRSA carrier's room have to wear a mask, gown, and gloves.

And so, Eyal was quarantined. His windows were firmly shut, and the door to his room was kept closed and marked with an orange "X," on orders of Infectious Disease Control.

To me, all this was excessive. Yes, MRSA was deadly, but was it really necessary to treat us like Biblical lepers? I could accept just about all the precautions, but the window thing, especially at the beginning of spring, drove me crazy. I found it hard to believe that Eyal's germs, if left unchecked, would float through a cracked window and contaminate the whole of upstate New York. The contrast between the glorious conditions outside and the stale oppression of Eyal's hospital room infuriated me. I stormed to the nurse's station to plead my case. The charge nurse, who by now had become a friend, looked up from her desk and asked if I needed anything.

"Yes," I said. "I'd like to open up Eyal's window to let in some fresh air. It's such a beautiful day."

The smile left her face. She took a stern, authoritative tone. "It can't be done. Because of the MRSA."

My body tensed. I tried to count to ten, but I only got as far as four. "Is there someone else I could please talk to?"

"Sure, but you'll get the same answer."

"That's okay. I still want to talk to someone."

I returned to Eyal's room. Several minutes later came the knock at the door. A nurse who worked in Infectious Disease Control beckoned me out into the hallway. A young woman with medium-length hair, she struck an imposing figure in her long white hospital coat. "I was told you had a question about the window." Before I could even open my mouth, she added, "It cannot be opened."

Clearly, the charge nurse had prepped her. She seemed ready for a fight. But so was I. I opened the door halfway and said, "Step in here, and feel what this room is like. It is a hot box." My voice rose a notch or two. "I don't understand how opening the window, even the slightest bit, will compromise the health of upstate New York. Please let me open the window, just a few inches."

She crossed her arms in front of her. "The MRSA rules are in place for the protection of *all* the patients in this hospital. Eyal is not the only patient."

"You're absolutely right," I said. "But he's my kid. And it's eighty-five degrees in there. It's unhealthy, unbearable. How is opening that window going to get anyone else sick?"

She furrowed her brow, feigning puzzlement. "Rabbi, how much do you know about MRSA?"

I'll admit it, I was furious. I physically towered over her and tried to intimidate her with my authoritative voice. "Listen, we're both reasonable people. Maybe I need to spell this out. I want that window opened. That little boy in there hasn't been outside in a year. *A year.* Maybe he will hear a bird, or a car honk, even a fire engine siren."

She shook her head. "I am sorry your son is sick. Again, I am responsible for *all* patients in this hospital."

I could see she wasn't going to bend the rules. Nothing was working. It was time to play my card. "Listen, the president of this hospital is a friend. I don't want to go there, but I want the window opened, at most six inches. That's all I want. Period."

I'm not sure if it was this threat that did the trick or if she finally saw the reasonableness of my position, but we agreed to a compromise: three inches.

By that time, an hour had passed. I was left with a little fresh air and my thoughts. I played the conversation over in my head, still trembling with rage. I couldn't believe the rigidity of this hospital. The nurse had been narrow-minded, to the point of stupidity. She hadn't been willing to give me a lousy six inches. Where do they get these people? Yet the ridiculousness of my own conduct seemed equally apparent. With everything happening in our lives, I had just done battle for more than an hour over a window! What had I been thinking? There had to be a better use of my energy and resources. I had won, but the victory was strangely unsatisfying.

By the late 1980s, once Eyal was home and our sense of crisis had dissipated, I came to understand better my reaction that day. My confrontation with the nurse hadn't been about the window. It had been about other things: victory and validation, ego, and most important, maintaining some sense of control in an environment where we had none. In the hospital, every single decision, from the timing of procedures and other treatments to when they mopped the floor, was made by someone else. Whether Eyal got better or worse, whether he lived or died, was out of my hands. I was feeling frustrated, guilty, and powerless. And angry.

Before Eyal had taken sick, I would get angry from time to time over petty things—not finding any milk in the fridge for my cereal, getting stuck in traffic, a work colleague who challenged me over where I parked my car. But after Eyal fell ill, I was constantly on edge. Raw emotion seethed just under the surface. The slightest intimidation, even unintended, pushed me to say or do something I would later regret. I was angry at the hospital for its silly and indiscriminate rules. I was angry with Leah for disagreeing with me over anything. I was angry with Eyal's doctors for not always listening and responding to my concerns. I was angry with the insurance company for making us jump through hoops. I was angry with our friends who didn't understand our pain and anguish. I was angry with members of my congregation who insisted I put their needs first. And I was angry at myself for not being able to "solve" this awful situation.

I'd like to say that God was the only one I wasn't angry at, but that's not entirely true. It felt like the walls were closing in. *Even God can't fix this*, I sometimes told myself in exasperation, intending the observation to be a kind of verbal assault on the Divine. I still believed in God. I continued to attend services and observe other Jewish rituals. But it was a while before my faith entirely outweighed my anger. Early on, my confusion, pain, and helplessness led me at especially difficult times to blame God for our misfortune, even as I continued to loyally perform my duties as a rabbi.

Whenever any of us are confronted with heartbreak and loss, we must find a way to process our anger. Whether it's justified or not, understandable or not, anger can be a formidable roadblock to healing. It can shut us down and lock us in. Left unaddressed, anger can poison all of our relationships, leaving us cynical, mean, and bitter. It can take hold of us body and soul and even threaten our faith. We can't learn to dream new dreams, find joy and happiness, or discover a new normal unless we first come to grips with our anger.

The life of Moses illustrates anger's destructive long-term consequences. The golden-calf episode was not the only time Moses expressed anger at his flock, the Israelites. During their forty years in the desert, the Israelites were constantly complaining. On one occasion, they complained that they lacked water and were thirsty. Moses, at the end of his rope, asked God to intercede. God directed Moses to a nearby rock and said that if Moses would only speak to the rock, refreshing and cool water would flow out of the rock to quench the people's thirst. The water would satisfy them physically and also give them a deeper faith. What happened? Moses didn't speak to the rock. He took his staff and smacked it in frustration. Water flowed out as promised, and a still-angry Moses yelled at the people, saying, "Hear now, you *rebels!*"

Moses had become so frustrated, vindictive, and out of control that he engaged in petty name-calling. And he paid a terrible price for this outburst. As a result of this one incident, God denied him entry into the Promised Land. The best Moses could look forward to, after forty years of schlepping this ungrateful people through the desert, was climbing a mountain and getting a look at the Promised Land.

Moses pleaded for another chance, but God denied his requests. Why? Because Moses still hadn't come to grips with his uncontrolled anger. He hadn't acknowledged how his anger affected him and his work as a leader. He hadn't accepted responsibility for his anger. In effect, Moses had locked himself in emotionally and spiritually and was no longer suited to lead his people. Moses's anger had undermined his dreams and his people's future, just as our anger undermines our own hopes, ambitions, and happiness.

I see evidence of anger's destructiveness all the time, especially at life-cycle events. Jewish tradition holds that when someone dies, friends and family should gather to console the mourners for seven days—what is called "sitting shiva"—at the home of a close relative. It's surprising how often I find myself announcing at the funeral that the family of the deceased will be holding two or three separate shivas, because, for example, Carol hasn't spoken to her sister Debbie in twenty years, and neither will set foot in the home of their brother Lenny. When I'm arranging a Bar or Bat Mitzvah, I will sometimes have to choreograph a service elaborately—who sits where, who stands where, who does what at what time—so that certain attendees who are estranged don't have to have the slightest social contact with one another. Often, the events that cause these estrangements are stunningly minor: an unintended slight, a word misused, an action misunderstood. Often, these events happened so long ago that the people involved don't even remember the details. But the pain and suffering of the estrangement, the biting bitterness, persists. And when children encounter this anger, new wounds open for another generation.

It's easy to say that we should all just "get over" our anger and move on. But sometimes that's not possible, no matter how hard we try. Sometimes our anger is legitimate. When we have suffered an egregious harm, when we've been lied to or betrayed, when something we value has been taken from us, when our spouses have cheated on us, when our business partners have stolen our life savings, when our kids have come down with a horrible disease, or when life just plain doesn't work out the way we imagined, we feel justified in our anger. We might simply lack the capacity to forgive and forget. What do we do then? Are we doomed to muddle along for the rest of our lives in bitterness? Will healing never come?

It seems to me that the first step to overcoming our anger is acknowledging it. If we make ourselves *aware* of our anger and its real, ultimate source—if we study our emotions and get in touch with them without feeling like we have to "solve" them right away—we can minimize their destructive impact, opening the way for healing to take place naturally, with the passage of time.

One way to stay in touch with our anger, so that time can work its magic, is to confront the person with whom we're angry. Years ago, a sexist commercial for aftershave showed an attractive woman going up to a man after he had shaved and slapping him angrily in the face. "Thanks," the man says, "I needed that!" Actually, we ourselves need to express our anger—not necessarily with a slap, but at least with words. No, the anger won't go away all at once, but at least we'll feel better after expressing it. This can make for a difficult conversation with another person, but it's better than wallowing in our anger, stewing in it, feeling like a victim, and then inventing elaborate justifications for it.

In 2011, the night before Thanksgiving, Eyal was admitted to a Syracuse hospital for a blood infection that had invaded his bones. He was in rough shape. His body was swollen from the infection, and doctors could not identify the bacteria at fault. Nobody was sure whether he'd pull out of it or not. To make matters worse, Leah and I were there all alone with him, since none of our other kids had come home for the holiday.

As we waited for the nurses to put an IV in Eyal's arm, Leah looked at me and sighed. "Well, another Thanksgiving in the ICU."

I smiled reassuringly. "At least someone will bring over dinner."

I had told a few leaders of my congregation about our situation, explaining that I needed time off from officiating at services to care for Eyal. I was confident someone from the synagogue would stop by with *something*, even just some turkey sandwiches or pumpkin pie. Our synagogue has always defined itself as a caring and compassionate community. On many occasions when congregants faced illness or a death in the family, we rallied behind them and provided help. Bringing Leah and me Thanksgiving dinner in the hospital seemed like a pretty obvious thing to do.

The next day, we waited and waited for our Thanksgiving dinner to arrive, but it never did. We never even received a phone call. I couldn't believe it. At 9 P.M., I threw up my hands and walked to the vending machines in the ICU waiting room. I bought every available package of M&M's. That was our Thanksgiving dinner. I spent the rest of the holiday confused, disappointed, and angry.

A few days later, Eyal responded to antibiotics. I went back to officiating at services, relieved but still very upset. My first inclination was to try to paper over my feelings and forget about what had happened. I decided against that. I knew that if I ignored how I felt, the anger would still be there, simmering below the surface and possibly poisoning my relationships. I wound up privately telling some congregational leaders how upset I was. I didn't try to embarrass them; I just informed them of what had happened. I knew I wasn't perfect. There were times when I myself had overlooked others in need. But on those occasions, I had at least owned up to my shortcomings. I hoped they would, too.

My friends offered no excuses. They sincerely apologized, and I felt much better. The mere act of expressing myself meant I didn't have to carry the negative feelings with me. I could move on. And what happened? A year later, when Eyal spent New Year's in the same hospital, we received a much better response. People called and sent unsolicited trays of food. The holiday still wasn't fun, but at least Leah and I felt cared for this time.

Many religions offer rituals of confession in which the faithful can express their anger, either in public or in private. As part of the Jewish ritual for divorce, a ceremony is held in which the decree of divorce issued by a Jewish court of law is presented to the woman whose marriage is ending. The woman takes the divorce decree in the palms of her hands and walks briefly around the room in the presence of others, expressing her feelings openly. Some women cry, others express anger. Sometimes husbands come, too, physically handling the divorce decree and presenting it to their wives. Judaism acknowledges that negative emotions like anger, pain, and loss are legitimate expressions of the human spirit, part of many life passages. Judaism sees it as best for people to let such emotions come out in a controlled, ritualized way, rather than hold them in and deny their existence.

We can also stay in touch with our anger—while mitigating its potential for harm—by consciously channeling it into positive action. Anger has the potential to help us do a lot of good in the world. Many of us become involved in community service or social organizations because something unfortunate happens that motivates us to change things. My own advocacy for those with special needs is not philosophical or theoretical but deeply, genuinely personal. Having a sick kid, I came to understand people with special needs like I never had before. My eyes had been opened. I took my anger and funneled it in a way that would be constructive and life affirming. In the process, I spent less time wallowing in resentment, self-pity, and victimhood.

It's important, too, to talk with a third party about your anger—a member of the clergy, a therapist, even a trusted friend. Express your anger, relive it, but also, over time, try to analyze and understand it, get to its roots and what it teaches you about yourself. Often, when we examine the source of our anger, our core beliefs about life, the world, and ourselves are revealed to us. Be as truthful as possible about the narratives you tell yourself. As a rabbi, I try to listen when congregants talk to me about their feelings of anger. It is not my place to persuade or dissuade them; I am there simply to listen. I ask questions to get them to talk about what happened, how it happened, why it happened. I am not a psychotherapist, and I don't expect my congregants to hold hands with me and experience a sudden resolution, a cathartic moment. But I do find that such conversations help people understand how they got to this point and what small, practical steps they can take to manage their anger.

The more we look our anger in the face, the more we can take steps to prevent it from flaring up and ensnaring us. Just as certain foods can exacerbate an underlying medical condition, so, too, can contact with certain situations or people inflame our emotions. We might not be able to change the source of our underlying anger, but we can purposely and consciously decide to avoid these irritating situations and people, for the sake of our own well-being. In so doing, we take back some measure of the control that we lose as victims. Resolving that we don't want to live our lives as angry, antisocial people, we steer ourselves onto a course that allows us to feel better.

Finally, I think it's important to remind ourselves along the way that the process of resolving our anger takes time. Sustaining unrealistic expectations about healing our emotions can lead to frustration, which makes the anger we feel even worse. In Judaism, theological arguments between schools of rabbis are quite bitter, often lasting hundreds of years. In recognition of the fact that sometimes we cannot resolve these disputes, Judaism has the concept of *teiku*—a tie. Nobody is right; there are no winners or losers. We'll learn the answer sometime in the future, when the Messiah comes. *Teiku* embodies the idea that we live in a world of tension, and we have to accept that some things will remain unresolved. So it is with anger. There may not be a solution today that satisfies us, but that is okay. One day, things will be different. We will feel less angry—and welcome life in more.

A Jewish folktale tells the story of a highly skilled jeweler who is working on a large, valuable diamond. He carves at first a beautiful rose, which further enhances the diamond's worth. He is proud of his workmanship and creativity. But then, distracted, he accidentally scratches the stone, making it flawed and ruining its value. The jeweler sits at his workbench, furious. He hangs his head in his hands and berates himself for his carelessness and inattentiveness. He casts about, looking for other people to blame. He is ready to throw out the diamond and disavow his hard work. He keeps staring at the diamond, the rose, at a loss for what to do. But after some time, as he calms down, he picks up his cutting tool and adds several leaves down the length of the scratch, making a stem for the rose, thus enhancing its original beauty.

It has taken me years, but as I have accepted my anger, looked it in the face, and done something with it, I have found that I have not only proceeded along the path of healing but created new beauty in my life. Understanding my own anger better has allowed me to empathize with others who are angry at me. I understand the deeper, hidden wounds that often manifest as discontent over specific issues. And rather than lash out defensively when confronted with anger, as I often did before Eyal took sick and in the early years of his illness, I am able to react in a more positive, healing way.

There was a family at the synagogue with children about the same age as Eyal. Their young adult daughter, a woman in her early thirties who was married with a toddler, living in the Midwest, passed away. She was accomplished and successful, a source of pride for the family and our community. I had officiated at all of her life-cycle passages. She had been sick for several years, an unusual cancer that kept recurring even with aggressive therapies. She fought courageously with the passionate support of her large family. During the latter course of her illness and immediately after she died, her parents were furious at me. We had several unpleasant conversations, and they really let me have it. "Rabbi, you weren't here for us," they told me. "We expected more from you. You knew how sick she was."

Initially, I took their criticisms personally, as an assault on my rabbinic professionalism. I felt defensive. I *had* reached out to them. I *had* called them. I *had* inquired with friends about how they were doing. I *had* said prayers in the synagogue for them. I wanted to reply to the family, forcing them to acknowledge all I had done for them. But then I thought a little more about what they were experiencing. Having dealt with my own anger issues for so long, I soon was able to get past my reaction. I didn't argue with them but instead just listened openly to their complaints. When I thought about it, I realized they were probably right. I had not been attentive *enough*. I had not called *enough*. I also asked myself, *What are they really saying to me? Are they really angry at me or at something else?* I could not have kept their daughter alive, but remembering my own encounter with Eyal's nurse, I sensed that a lot of their anger came from their realization that no one could have. They were upset at their own helplessness and powerlessness, just as I had been at mine. Maybe they even saw me as the agent of a God who had abandoned them.

Another story comes to mind. During the first year or two after Eyal got sick, we received thousands of letters and cards conveying sentiments like, "We're thinking about you," "You and Eyal are in our prayers," and "Please let us know if we can help." While we appreciated the thought and caring of the senders, we wound up putting those cards and letters in cartons and storing them in our basement. But one letter, on a monogrammed, ivory note card, handwritten in dark blue ink, never made it into a carton. I keep it in the top right-hand drawer of my desk in my home study. I have read and reread this letter many times.

It was from an older woman who at one time was very active and engaged in my synagogue. This woman had never been a fan of mine, not because of anything I had done or hadn't done, but because when I arrived as the new young rabbi, I replaced the older rabbi who had been her favorite. He had been with her through the illness and death of her teenage daughter many years earlier, and thcy had been very close.

"Dear Rabbi Sherman," her letter began, "I've already noticed over the holidays from what you have experienced, it has made you a more gentle, kind person. It has made you a better rabbi."

For years after I received this letter, I was surprised at how much the words continued to upset me. I was furious and hurt. The problem wasn't merely her contention that I used to be a less kind and gentle person, but rather her suggestion that it took Eyal's misfortunes for me to morph into the kind of rabbi she wanted. No one should have to learn that kind of life lesson from their child nearly dying. I would have much preferred to have Eyal well than to be the gentle, generous, warm, fuzzy rabbi this woman wanted.

This letter became just one more thing for me to be angry about. But eventually I came to understand it better. First, the letter contained some truth. I had changed. Second, she had not written the letter maliciously; she hadn't meant to hurt me. She herself had traveled down this same painful path, but she was farther along. Only later did I learn that in response to her young daughter's untimely death she and her family had established a foundation to fund research to find a cure for the genetic disease that afflicted her daughter. At some time during her journey, this woman must have decided to take her anger and her pain and do something positive with it. It must have been difficult for her to sit down and write me a letter that she thought would offer me comfort and encouragement. But I never wrote back. I purposefully avoided any kind of one-on-one interaction with her. She has since passed away, and I am sorry I never told her what she taught me.

All of us who are angry and who have trouble dealing with it are in good company. The Bible has a lot of anger in it; it isn't just Moses. Sarah and Hagar fight so bitterly that Sarah convinces her husband, Abraham, to throw out Hagar, Abraham's consort, and Hagar's son, Ishmael. Jacob and Esau become bitter enemies; for decades Jacob lives fearing that his brother might come and kill him. Joseph's brothers are so angry that their father has taken him as his favorite that they sell him into slavery. And of course, God is angry—at Moses, at the Israelites, at Adam and Eve, at the generation of Noah, at the twin cities of Sodom and Gomorrah.

Interestingly, we don't see a lot of reconciliation in the Bible. This is not *Ozzie and Harriet*. These Biblical characters live unresolved lives. They do the best they can with what they have. Sometimes they succeed in putting issues behind them, but I believe that the value in these stories is the lessons they teach about how to live with anger even when it burns hot and unremitting. And so it is with us today. Do the best you can to resolve what unsettles you, and realize that anger is an essential part of the human condition. Above all, stay hopeful. As God reminds us, His anger is not forever. He is capable of forgiveness. And since we humans are created in God's image, we can forgive, too. It just might take a little while. As we carry the broken and the whole together with us, let us consider how the broken includes these as-yet-unhealed feelings of anger.

Regret

A family I knew seemed to have everything. They were well-off, grounded, very nice people. Several years ago, they flew to another state to celebrate their parents' golden wedding anniversary. The oldest son, a freshman in college, borrowed the rental car to see some friends. His parents insisted he be back to his grandparents' home by 6 P.M., not a minute later, to take family photographs. For reasons that remain unknown, the son lost control of the car, flipped it, and was killed. The family was devastated, inconsolable. Months later, they were still incapacitated by grief. One year went by, another year. They continued to withdraw from the community.

The parents blamed themselves for what had happened to their son. They believed that if they hadn't insisted that he be back by 6 P.M., or if they had not allowed him to drive in an unfamiliar city, he wouldn't have died. Carrying this burden, they could no longer sustain healthy and necessary human relationships. All energy and life was sucked out of them, and they wanted only solitude in their pain and grief. Somehow they felt that forgiving themselves amounted to disloyalty to their son, when in fact their responsibility for what happened was uncertain at best. Regret consumed them, to the point where living with it became not really living at all.

I've spoken of anger toward others; what about the negative emotions we feel toward ourselves when our normal life and dreams are shattered? How do we resolve self-inflicted pain?

It's easy to second-guess ourselves—"I should have done this," "What if I had done that?" So often we beat ourselves up, wondering in retrospect how we might have used our powers to prevent disaster. Although understandable, such thinking only makes things worse. To the extent that we fail to confront our regrets head-on, we remain caught in the past and the pain, hurt, and trauma of what has happened. We fail to live as fully as we might in the present. Any joy or happiness we might feel in our new circumstances goes unexplored, and we never regain a sense of comfort, wholeness, or normalcy.

Jewish tradition contains mechanisms for overcoming regret. The holy day of Yom Kippur serves as an occasion for Jews to express remorse to the Creator by confessing their sins and transgressions. At the beginning of the holy day, right before sunset, the community comes together to publicly disavow all promises between God and human beings made in the previous year. The blackboard is erased, and we start anew in our spiritual lives. This new beginning is hopeful and life affirming.

At the beginning of the holy day, Jews repeat a phrase from the Book of Numbers in which God speaks to Moses, saying, "I have pardoned them." You would think that this phrase would be repeated at the *end* of the holy day, after the twenty-five-hour fast of contrition and repentance. But instead, this statement is made at the beginning of the holy day. Why are Jews symbolically forgiven at the outset?

The answer is simple. From the very start, God forgives the penitents for their misdeeds. Then, during the period of fasting, the penitents begin the work of trying to forgive *themselves*. The easy part of processing what we have done is Divine forgiveness. The truly torturous part is *self-forgiveness* and the overcoming of our internal regrets.

For years, I berated myself about Eyal's illness. It had not come out of nowhere. There had been signs. By the time Eyal was a toddler, his voice was unusually raspy, sounding more like a heavy smoker's than a little boy's. He tired easily; a run around the bases during baseball games left him out of breath. He had those terrible mood swings—silly and laughing one minute, defiant and slamming doors the next. We were always taking him to the pediatrician with the same symptoms: low-grade temperature, congestion, pain in his right ear so intense he would yank out chunks of hair. Each time, the doctor gave us an antibiotic or some other symptomatic treatment and said, "Don't worry, this is normal. He'll outgrow this."

After Eyal received his devastating diagnosis of a brainstem lesion, his pediatrician approached me in the intensive care unit. "Rabbi, I heard the bad news. It would not have made any difference if Eyal had been diagnosed earlier." I have replayed those words—"It would not have made any difference"—countless times in my mind. Was that his honest medical judgment? Was he saying this to protect his reputation? Was he trying to ease my conscience?

Leah and I had three other young children; we had

known what normal childhood physical development looked like. Should we have been more aggressive about Eyal's early care? Shouldn't we have taken Eyal to get a second opinion, even using my professional connections to get a well-known specialist to check him out? If we had been more thorough, would we have caught the lesion earlier, and if we had, would more treatment options have been available? Would Eyal's surgery have been necessary? Would he have suffered that devastating stroke? Would things have been different?

I used to beat myself up over these questions. No matter how hard I tried to rationalize our actions, the questions would come up again. Like that grieving family who lost their son, I withdrew into myself, staying far below the surface. I felt dirty, soiled. I walked around all day long with a knot in my stomach and in my chest. I kept telling myself, *It didn't have to be this way*. Out of guilt, I would sometimes burst into action, getting on the phone and following a lead, researching some medical advance someone had told me about—all to no avail. Then, for long stretches of time, I felt bruised and defeated. My emotions were strangling me, sucking the life out of me. I didn't know how to make them stop.

I often give pastoral advice to people tormented by painful life circumstances for which they feel responsible. Before Eyal's illness, I used to tell them simply, "You need to let it go, get over it, move on." I thought this was working. People would thank me for my advice and they wouldn't schedule a follow-up visit, which I assumed meant they had resolved their internal conflicts and moved on. I'd congratulate myself on a job well done.

Now that I have been at the receiving end of this advice,

I realize that those people had not moved on. I had failed them. I had not appreciated the depth of their pain and hurt. "Move on" is not what a lot of us want to hear. "Move on" doesn't do anybody any good. I was not providing any kind of meaningful healing insight to help them deal with their guilt or regret.

Today, as I place my son in a Hoyer lift, or suction his lungs with a catheter, or wipe saliva from his chin, I still wonder if I could have done more for him. But these thoughts don't dominate my life. I have learned over time to acknowledge my regret and live with it, just as I have done with my anger toward others. It got a lot easier when I stopped trying to "get over" my feelings and started asking how I could reach a working accommodation with them.

Over the years, I have tried to be honest with myself and accept that we made decisions that I regret. I force myself to be very specific about what we did or did not do. We did not pay close enough attention to Eyal's symptoms. We let things slide. We listened to Eyal's doctor because it had been convenient to do so and he was "the boss." I live with these realities. They are part of who I am. I am an imperfect human. I cannot put my life through the laundry and get out the stain.

But acknowledging this is the beginning of the healing process. We can't heal unless we have first identified the source of our pain and confusion, and that means self-discovery and honest acceptance of what went wrong and what our role was. We can't forgive ourselves until we are clear on what we need forgiveness for.

Moving from acceptance to forgiveness to healing does not mean that I never experience pangs of guilt. Occasionally, when I am alone in the car, or shaving in the morning, or sitting in my leather recliner late at night, the pain hits me from out of nowhere, and it hurts. When I see a kid who went to school with Eyal, when I hear about what that kid is doing in his life—starting a family, getting a new job, making an exciting move across the country—I feel a blow to my chest. A voice goes off inside me: "Eyal will never have that." The same thing happens when I think about the lives my other children are leading. But because I have done the work of admitting my failings to myself, I don't get sucked down into a vortex of despair.

Other tactics also help me to carry the regret with me in my daily life. I force myself to remain active and absorbed (some say preoccupied) so that my dark moments don't get out of control. My work serves as a welcome outlet, a necessary escape, more avocation than vocation. It fills the hours and keeps me from lingering in that "bad place" too long. The more I keep my mind and body engaged, minimizing the empty time that leads to wallowing in self-pity and regret, the better off I find myself.

Eyal still requires enormous care; he has no real friends except his siblings and Leah and me. Helping Eyal engage in the world beyond his hospital bed and medical equipment also keeps me active, engaged—and happy. Every day, I look for something for Eyal to do: a drive to the local mall, an afternoon at a county park, a visit to a big bookstore, a trip to the local art museum. I read him the newspaper every day. Leah does crossword puzzles with him. It keeps him busy and helps all three of us stay sane.

We also make a conscious effort to learn from the past and not repeat our mistakes. In my case, I have tried to make more informed and deliberate decisions about Eyal's health, not accepting at face value what doctors or other "experts" tell us.

In 1998, when Eyal was suffering from profound scoliosis, the doctors told us, "Eyal's back is like a question mark. It compromises the function of many of his internal organs. They are squashed. He needs an intervention right now." Eyal was so physically challenged and immune compromised that a major surgery like the one needed to correct his scoliosis could have killed him.

Rather than simply say, "Okay, doctor, we'll do whatever you advise," I took the time to do serious research. I worked the phones, calling anyone who might have been able to counsel me on the decision, asking questions, and taking copious notes. I had Eyal's charts sent to doctors outside Syracuse. And then I went to talk to the doctors in person. I drove six and a half hours to Wilmington, Delaware, and returned the same day. A few days later, I drove to New York City and grilled a different specialist. A couple of days after that, I drove to and from Toronto. Perhaps my research was a little excessive, but I didn't care. If Eyal was to go under the knife, I wanted to be damn sure it would be under the supervision of the right doctor, in the right hospital, in the right city. We would do whatever it took to get the best results.

Eyal ended up having the surgery at a hospital outside Syracuse that specialized in pediatric orthopedics. It was a disaster. An infection broke out a week or so after the procedure; treating it required a hospital admission of several months, three additional surgeries, and months of antibiotic therapy. But this time, I didn't regret any of my actions before the surgery. I knew I had left no stone unturned. It was excruciating for Leah and me to see our son so sick, but I took solace in the fact that we had done the absolute best we could.

This more cautious, thoughtful way of making decisions

has spilled into my professional and personal life. I used to respond impulsively to any problem that came my way. Frequently, the ill-considered decisions I embraced or advised others to make ended up causing more problems later on. I would come away regretting words I had chosen, the tone of voice I had taken with people. But I have learned from my regret. Now, unless it is an absolute emergency, I use these simple phrases: "Let me think about it a little while. I'll get back to you." The extra time allows for some distance and context, an opportunity to examine different facets of an issue. Occasionally, it lets me cool down. Not surprisingly, my responses tend to be better, and so are the outcomes.

There is a middle ground between simply forgetting the past, so as to move on, and replaying the past so often and so negatively that you can never escape it. When we look at the Bible, we find support for this balance. On the one hand, the Bible exhorts us to remember the past, most notably in Jewish rituals, holidays, and ceremonies. During the Passover Seder, the ceremonial dinner, Jews retell the story of the Exodus and the ten plagues. Every Friday evening, while saying a blessing over the wine, Jews remind themselves of creation. During the Purim holiday, Jews publicly recall the ancient story of the evil Haman and the wicked Amalekites.

Yet the Bible also stakes out important limits to our remembrance of the past. Consider the story of Lot, Abraham's nephew, and his wife, the unnamed Mrs. Lot. They live in the wicked twin cities of Sodom and Gomorrah. God decides that these cities harbor such insidious evil that He has to destroy them. Abraham, gentle soul that he is, stalwart of fairness and goodness, goes toe to toe with God. How dare

God destroy the whole population of these cities—the good people and the bad ones together?

Well, it turns out that the only good people in Sodom and Gomorrah are Lot, Mrs. Lot, and their kids. The die has been cast; the city is to be destroyed. As Lot and his wife leave the city for the last time, God instructs them, "Don't look back." Mrs. Lot disregards that instruction; she takes a final look back and becomes, in popular parlance, a pillar of salt, frozen for all eternity. I can understand why she was told not to look back; probably God thought there was nothing to be gained from fixating on the past.

Eyal's narrative, painful as it is, always remains with me as a point of reference, especially during harder times. But thanks to the tactics I've described, I don't think of it as the central focus of who I am and what I am about. And as time has passed, the sting of regret has diminished.

If we hang in there and do the hard, ongoing work of staying in that middle ground, we can hold out hope to one day find what we crave: total self-forgiveness in our hearts, and the deep, satisfying resolution of our feelings of regret. Avi Weiss, a prominent rabbi, educator, and political activist, knows this well. He has described publicly the pain he experienced upon losing a four-month-old son to a rare genetic disease. He was so distraught that he couldn't bring himself to visit his son's grave for many years. As time passed, he came to feel guilty for not visiting. Finally he decided to go, so he called the cemetery and tried to locate the burial plot. The cemetery told him there was no plot assigned to his son; maybe the baby was buried elsewhere. Heartbroken once again, Weiss visited the cemetery in person and called others who might have had some knowledge of his son's burial location, all to no avail.

Many years passed. One day, Weiss received a request to perform a ceremony at the cemetery where he initially had thought his son was buried. Stopping at the cemetery's office, he asked to look at their records himself. When the administrators refused, claiming that they didn't allow access to such confidential information, Weiss broke down in tears. They relented, and Weiss went through the handwritten cemetery records line by line (this was before computerized files). He did indeed find his son's grave listed; his first name and middle name had been reversed. Weiss resolved to visit his son's grave that year several days before Yom Kippur and put a stone on it.

He couldn't bring himself to do it. A few more years passed. Finally, a close friend heard of his difficulty and offered to go with him. Weiss and his wife visited the grave for the first time, some forty years after their son had passed.

As they stood near the stone, Weiss read its inscription: "Is not Ephraim my precious son, my darling child?" His wife cleared off the stone as if making a bed for her infant son. Weiss whispered to his son, "I am so sorry that I am late. I love you."

And in response, Rabbi Weiss is convinced he heard his son say, "It's okay, Abba, it's okay. I love you, too!"

I am not sure Avi Weiss actually heard his son utter those words, although I pray to God he did. I think the voice he heard was his own voice, an inner voice, saying to him, "It's okay. I forgive you." All of us want to hear words like those. We all want to forgive ourselves, for whatever we have done or not done, and most of all, for not being perfect.

Time

∞

A daily practice of feeling thankful for what we have doesn't just alert us to life's good things, it also helps to alter our perception of time, so that we appreciate the present moment. It's harder to grieve for what has happened and worry about what might happen if we're focused on noticing the sunrise and feeling grateful for just having woken up. We can move closer to the Promised Land after a disaster if we learn to linger more in the present and savor what *is*.

Prior to Eyal's health problems, I had always been a tomorrow kind of guy. In elementary school, I wanted to be in junior high school. In junior high school, I wanted to be in high school. In high school, I wanted to be in college. In college, I wanted to be in rabbinical school. When I was an assistant rabbi, I wanted to be senior rabbi. Just about everything had to do with tomorrow's time. And always being on tomorrow's time translated into being an impatient person. It was as if anything happening today was irrelevant.

All that began to change in March 1986, during Eyal's initial hospital admission, when he underwent the invasive, life-threatening surgery to reduce the size of his lesion. The doctors told us the surgery would last fourteen hours. Every few minutes, I glanced at my watch. Time moved agonizingly slowly. I wanted this thing to be over. Never had the present been so difficult to endure; never did I think in terms of future time more than I did then. When fourteen hours had passed, the doctors still weren't finished. It took them three additional hours, the slowest hours of all, before we were finally summoned.

We met in a large conference room and spoke to the neurosurgeon and resident surgeon who had operated on Eyal. The doctors, still dressed in their baby-blue scrubs, had grim looks on their exhausted faces.

"It's what I thought," the neurosurgeon said. "Preliminary pathology suggests an astrocytoma, pediatric glioma, grade two." He spoke quickly, fidgeting with his hands. "A very large benign lesion, the size of a golf ball, at the junction of the brain stem and cervical spinal cord. It is in a horrible place, not on but inside the brain stem."

Finding a napkin on a nearby table, the surgeon sketched out the brain stem and the placement of Eyal's lesion. "It's already done significant damage to Eyal's ability to maintain a good heart rate and sustain a satisfactory breathing effort. The best I could do was debulk a small percentage of the lesion. When I tried to be more aggressive, Eyal's blood pressure began to drop dangerously. He will be on a ventilator." Leah stared coldly into the distance. Her body trembled.

"There are no surgical options," the surgeon said. "Any further attempt to remove the lesion likely will kill him right away or make him so physically compromised that there would be no quality of life."

My heart fell into my stomach. I thought he was talking about someone else. My mouth opened to say something, but nothing came out. Finally, I found the words. "How much time does he have?"

"Excuse me?" the doctor asked, cocking his ear to the side. I had spoken softly, almost inaudibly.

"How much time does he have?"

The doctor shrugged. "With radiation treatments, twelve months. Maybe."

Suddenly, time stood utterly still. I reached for a chair and motioned gently for Leah to sit. "Could you please bring us a glass of cold water?" I asked the resident.

Leah was thirty-five years old, with brown shoulder-length hair, warm eyes, a soft and beautiful smile. She was expecting our fifth child in three months. I wondered what all of this would do to her. It was a terrible contradiction: a new life grew within her body, while at the same time, the child she'd once carried withered in a hospital bed.

The resident returned with the water, and my thoughts turned to Eyal. How do you gauge twelve months in the life of a kid? Is it how tall he will grow? How much weight he will gain? How long his hair will become? How many baby teeth of his will fall out? Or perhaps the benchmarks relate to experiences and milestones. Will he learn to ride a bicycle? Will he learn to read? Will he start Hebrew school?

If the doctors were right, Eyal would miss out on so much. His first kiss. Falling in love. Having his Bar Mitzvah. Going to high school. Graduating from college. Getting married. Having kids of his own.

The door to the conference room partially opened, and in the hallway beyond I spotted a stretcher moving briskly down the tile floor. Three or four nurses surrounded it, as well as a respiratory therapist, a couple of doctors, IV poles, a ventilator, and a heart monitor. It was hard to see who the patient was at first but then, still through the crack in the door, I realized it was Eyal.

Leah and I ran to the hall. I expected that Eyal would look horrible, but his cheeks were rosy, his eyes bright and open. He was awake and focused. I had asked that they not shave his head entirely, for I saw his strawberry-blond hair as a symbol of his dignity and humanity. They assured us they would do their best, given the surgical cut's location at the back of his skull. They were true to their word. The back of his head rested on a pillow, protected by a large white bandage. Hair still covered most of his head; spiked with gel, it was a young man's haircut, and it looked surprisingly good. I found myself thinking that seventeen hours ago we'd said good-bye to a young toddler, and now in many ways, he was returning to us a man. It's not age or a particular number that defines maturity or adulthood. It is life experience. I know a lot of people who are technically adults but live as children. There are others, like Eyal, who, because of what they have experienced or heard, quickly become mature and wise beyond their years.

The ventilator did not allow Eyal to speak. We read his lips. A simple question: "What happened to today?"

I was surprised that after such a long surgery, Eyal was able to engage us in conversation. I thought he would be sedated for hours. But it was this question that really startled me. What exactly was he asking? Did he want to know the details of how long he had been asleep? Or was he really trying to say that the day was gone, and with it his childhood, and he'd never get it back?

Time works in strange ways. It does not chug along at regular intervals, like a moving sidewalk, ushering us from one moment to the next, one appointment or activity to the next. Rather, it is layered and multifaceted. It can seem to stop and then rush ahead, all at once. When we were told Eyal had only twelve months to live, it was as though time stopped. But when he came out of surgery, more relaxed, more comfortable, more grown-up, it was as though time had sped up, ushering him into an early adulthood. We can't control time or have expectations about it. We have to accept its mysterious ways and live in each moment as it is given to us.

Two nurses pushed Eyal's stretcher down the hall. Leah and I walked alongside, holding his hands. "Mom and Dad, you'll have to wait outside a few minutes, we'll get you as soon as possible," a nurse told us as we arrived at the PICU. "He'll be fine."

Leah and I were relieved but drained and scared. Hand in hand, we walked in silence back to the parents' room. I reached for my watch, an old Timex with a large face and well-worn dark brown leather strap. It was a gift from my mother and father when I graduated from rabbinical school. I always wore it. In the shower, swimming, to bed. As always, it was set five minutes ahead.

I unfastened the band and placed the watch in my pants pocket, telling myself I was putting it away forever.

In 1993, when Eyal graduated from elementary school and was about to move on to middle school, I asked him if he was afraid. The change meant new teachers, a new building, a new aide, different homework demands. He thought for a moment. "I'm scared," he told me. I tried to reassure him, telling him that it would be easier to get to his new school, it was a bigger building, the teachers would be nice. He didn't say exactly what he feared. I think what he was saying was that he wanted to stay in the present, where he was comfortable. He was sick and fragile and had all kinds of challenges, but he had learned to live with those challenges. And he was not sure what the future would hold.

Fourteen years later, in 2007, we had a similar conversation. His immediate older sister, Orah, had gotten engaged. She was the first of the kids to get married. After her wedding, she would move to London with her husband, David. I discussed the wedding plans with Eyal, who said, "Things are going too fast." Once again, I did not understand at first what he was telling me, but when I thought about it, I realized that maybe he was upset that everyone was going forward into the future, moving along with their lives, and because of his "situation," as he calls it, he was feeling left behind.

It is the nature of life that no one knows what the next moment will bring. Thus, we are called to cherish the moments in time that we experience today. The past is gone, and the future may never happen. We only have this moment.

The Bible's fourth book, the Book of Numbers, narrates the Israelites' forty-year trek from Egyptian bondage through the desert to the Promised Land. In a text where each word is significant and valued, the Book of Numbers contains long chapters that read like MapQuest directions, chronicling the desert experience. "The children of Israel journeyed from Rameses and pitched their tents in Succoth. They journeyed from Succoth and pitched their tents in Etham." These details don't add much to the narrative, but they do speak to what I think life is really all about. It's a *journey* to a Promised Land; life *is* the wandering in the desert. The present moment matters—not our future destination. And maybe that's why when we come to the end of the Five Books of Moses, the Israelites are still in the desert, catching only a glimpse of the Promised Land.

One member of my congregation, a very successful man in his mid-sixties, rarely came to services. One day, he developed a life-threatening heart problem and traveled to Boston, Mass General, for risky surgery, scheduled, of all days, on Yom Kippur, the holiest day of the Jewish year. He made it through the surgery well. Afterward, he began attending services every Saturday morning.

I never asked him about this change in behavior, but I imagine that while he was lying on the operating table, right before they put him under, he had a conversation with God. "I don't know what is going to happen," he might have said. "I have squandered a lot of opportunities in my life, wasted time that could have been spent on making myself a better person, helping my family, helping others. Get me through this surgery, God, and I will reorder my priorities. I will slow down and appreciate the time I have. I will enjoy the Sabbath as it is meant to be enjoyed—as a time to reflect and take a deep breath in the moment."

The past can overwhelm our ability to live in the present moment and make something good out of our lives. And sometimes the future can control us; we lose ourselves working toward some vague, obscure goal, or we become terrified of losing what we have or of giving up our dreams. Somehow, this congregant of mine had come to understand that his time on this earth was finite and decided that if he got a second chance, he would get it right. Every moment he was alive would have meaning for him. He would appreciate the *journey* of life.

Milton Steinberg was the rabbi during the 1930s and '40s at New York City's Park Avenue Synagogue, the most prestigious pulpit in North America. In a now-celebrated and famous sermon, Steinberg recounted having suffered at age forty a major heart attack while visiting Jewish troops at a Texas military base. He was absolutely certain he was dying. After a long, hard recovery, he took his first walk out of the hospital. "The sky overhead was very blue, very clear and very, very high . . . And in that instant, I looked about me, to see if anyone else showed on his face, the joy, the beatitude I felt, but no, there they walked, men and women and children in the glory of the golden flood, and so far as I could detect, there was none to give it heed. And then I remembered how often I too had been indifferent to sunlight, how often preoccupied with petty and sometimes mean concerns, I had disregarded it. And I said to myself, how precious is the sunlight, but alas, how careless of it are men, how precious— how careless. This has been a refrain sounding in me ever since."

Steinberg exhorted his listeners to enjoy the moment and spend their time wisely, purposefully. Each day gives us the opportunity to discover healing and accomplishment. The journey of life, granted to us by our Creator, is magnificent indeed.

People ask me all the time, "How are you doing? How is everything? How is Eyal?" My answer, from years of living with our reality, is, "*Today* is pretty good."

Psalm 118 proclaims: "*This* is the day the Lord has made;

let us rejoice and be glad" (emphasis mine). No specifics are offered, no reasons given. Why is this day so deserving of celebration and exultation? I can't believe that every day is productive, full of warm sunshine, good health, accomplishment, even fun. What the psalmist is saying, through the prism of time, is that we should count whatever blessings we have. Enjoy this day. Nothing is said about yesterday's time, tomorrow's time. It's about today's time.

Today, Leah and I continue to live in the present. We don't just try to get through the day, flipping our calendar pages to see what's on for tomorrow. We don't know how much time Eyal and we have together; nobody knows. All we know is that we have this moment.

Acts of Loving-kindness

∞

By May 1987, we had been in the Syracuse hospital for close to six months, and Eyal had just turned six. He wasn't doing well. He remained tethered to a ventilator, and apart from some chemotherapy, he was not receiving any treatment. No one expected, or certainly promised, any further recovery. A G-tube had been placed in his belly. He never got dressed. And because of his MRSA infection, he had no interaction with the rest of the floor or the hospital. He was in isolation. Occasionally, physical and occupational therapists visited. Once or twice a day, nurses and orderlies picked him up and placed him in a bedside lounge chair.

Amidst all this, a new face appeared on the floor, a youthful grandmother, early sixties, tall and elegant. She was dressed carefully in sedate browns and earth tones. Her once-black hair was peppered with gray and pulled back in a stylish French knot, her makeup subtle. She was already the *yente*, the good-natured busybody, of the fourth floor, interested in learning everybody's business. Her thirteen-year-old granddaughter was on four north, the less acute side of the pediatric floor, awaiting a tonsillectomy.

As her granddaughter napped, Grandmom took her

usual midafternoon stroll down the hall, through both the north and south sides, stopping at almost every door and unabashedly peeking in before continuing. When she arrived at our doorway, she made no effort to hide her interest in Eyal's story. In fact, she moved a foot or two closer to the door to get a better view.

Although Eyal was paralyzed, unable to hold anything in his hands, he kept asking for a box of crayons. The grandmother could only hear my side of the conversation, but she put together the story. Eyal wanted to play tic tac toe. I should use the crayons to draw the board, the X's and O's. He was very specific and demanding. Eyal mouthed to me that he wanted bright dazzling colors. Not just your basic eight-color pack, but the kind with several rows and dozens of colors—Prussian blue, burnt sienna, ochre yellow.

We heard a knock on the door. "I couldn't help but hear your conversation," the grandmother said. "May I please buy him the crayons?"

At first, I was irritated, thinking it inappropriate for "Mrs. Busybody" or anybody else to eavesdrop on a private conversation. "No, no, please," I said, waving her off. "You're very kind, but that's not necessary. Thanks for your offer."

But this lady without a name, the grandmother of the kid awaiting a tonsillectomy, would not take no for an answer. She raised her right hand as if she was stopping traffic. "I'd like to do it, please. I'm on my way to the gift shop anyway."

I don't remember what I said, but twenty minutes later, she returned with crayons in more colors than we thought existed. She also brought back the latest popular toy craze, a Pound Puppy. He was cute and cuddly, dark brown, with fluffy, adorable ears, oversized paws, a little tail, and a Pound Puppy symbol sewn into his backside. I reached for my wallet to reimburse her, but she again raised her hand, shaking her head and letting me know, in no uncertain terms, that this was a gift. I was at once embarrassed, surprised, and grateful. Eyal didn't know what to make of the gesture, but he was thrilled that he got all of the crayons and an unexpected toy dog. I rubbed it against his cheek. "Eyal, thank the nice lady for the presents."

"Thank you," Eyal dutifully mouthed.

Like expressing gratitude and living in the moment, performing acts of loving-kindness can, over time, catapult us to new heights of healing and contentment, even as we continue to carry brokenness within us. In fact, a thankful, present-centered mentality goes hand in hand with loving-kindness. When we're living in the moment, aware of what we've been given, we naturally become more alert to others and their needs. Our hearts open, and we are moved to help. The more action we take, the more our hearts open. It's a gradual process. Slowly, we discover a light in people we never saw before, one that makes life seem increasingly worth living. And sometimes, we discover that same light of goodness in ourselves.

But can we feel capable of helping others when we're already hurting? It's more natural than we might think. When disaster strikes, unexpected generosity bestowed on us by others can cause the seeds of loving-kindness to germinate and take root. I know from experience.

The grandmother who brought Eyal the puppy and the crayons had every reason to remain absorbed in her granddaughter's challenge, to shut herself off to the suffering of others. And I would have understood, because that's exactly what I was doing. I did not have the energy or the desire to concern myself with anyone except Eyal and my family. I did what I had to do in the synagogue, the minimum to get by, and that was it. But this woman was only one in an endless parade of good people who surfaced in the hospitals we visited. Unannounced and unanticipated, they emerged to lend a helping hand, expecting no compensation, recognition, or pats on the back.

I was continually surprised by people like the Santa Clauses of all shapes, sizes, genders, and ethnic persuasions who showed up before Christmas to sing carols and pass out treats. The Easter Bunnies, clowns, magicians, Halloween goblins, cartoon characters. Then there were those who brought in their dogs, knowing that petting a gentle animal can bring a smile to a child's face and help to break up the day. There were musicians who toted guitars and keyboards, older women who pushed the candy cart down the hall or offered a cold beverage to tired and thirsty parents.

During the early years of Eyal's illness, when a volunteer clown visited, I said to myself, *Cute, that's nice*, and dismissed it as an isolated event. But Eyal has been in five major hospitals over the last twenty-five years, usually for long periods of time. What I discovered is that volunteer clowns—and volunteers of all kinds—are not an anomaly. They are the norm. And each of these volunteers was a caring soul who had paid the parking fee in the garage, waited for the elevator, and taken time out of his or her day to give a moment of joy to an unknown sick kid.

It wasn't just volunteers who went out of their way to show loving-kindness, but staff members, too. At times I would lose patience with the hospital community, feeling they did not understand our needs. *It's a job for them*, I thought. But then there were moments when I witnessed quiet acts of generosity and kindness. I remember a little toddler named April who had resided at the Syracuse hospital since birth. Nobody ever came to visit this kid. She just lay in a large white metal crib in a corner room. Over time, I came to learn that she had been born with multiple problems: stunted growth, an unusually large head, impaired vision, no apparent intellectual abilities. She was ventilator dependent, tube fed, catheterized every four hours.

The staff hoped that one of these days she would be transferred to a state-run institution for a "more normal life experience." But in the meantime, she had been abandoned. And yet, not entirely. Several times a week, April's nurses grabbed a hospital laundry bag and filled it with her dirty laundry: stained hospital gowns, bibs, washcloths, little socks. Instead of using the hospital laundry service, the nurses took turns bringing the laundry home and washing it in their own machines, returning it the next day fluffy and soft, with the scent of fresh lemons. It was not just clean; it had been washed with love.

Besides that grandmother in the hospital, another person who really came through for us was a respiratory therapist we worked with in 1988, when we were about to have Eyal come back to live at home. It had taken more than six months of careful planning and preparation to pull it off, and he would be one of the first kids in such a fragile condition to leave a hospital setting. Planning his homecoming had been quite an exercise. We had to coordinate between the nursing agencies, the respiratory therapist, and the medical-supply companies. A date was picked: Monday, September 14. We needed all of the medical services in place by then; everyone needed to be on call in case a problem arose. Our minds were set on that date, which coincidentally was the evening of Rosh Hashanah. We were focused in on it. We couldn't wait. And we had told Eyal it was coming. But we were scared to death that something would go wrong.

A couple days before Eyal's discharge, something did. The respiratory therapist bounced into the room and asked, "Have you decided what day will be discharge day?"

"Nobody told you?" I asked. "It's this coming Monday. Early in the morning."

Her face fell and her body froze. "I'm getting married this weekend. I'll be on my honeymoon. There's no one else who can cover. Only I know all of Eyal's needs."

We parted company with all of our plans up in the air. Leah and I didn't know what to do. After all that we had been through, all the preparations we had made, we couldn't bear to wait another day. And changing the date would have required endless calls and negotiations to coordinate all over again the many nurses, specialists, and others involved in the transition. It was almost too much to contemplate. And Eyal was so excited to be going home. We didn't want to disappoint him.

It turned out we didn't have to worry. Later that day, I got a call from the respiratory therapist. In an almost breathtaking display of loving-kindness, she said, "You don't need to worry about Eyal. I'll be there Monday." And come Monday, the big day, there she was.

Why did she change her honeymoon plans? I never asked. Nor did I ask for an explanation from the countless others who went beyond the "call of duty" to help us. It's sad to say, but part of me assumed they had ulterior motives—that their charity was self-serving, sort of like, "Look at me, look what I'm doing." Or maybe they were helping out because it filled an empty space in their lives. Or because they were trying to puff up a résumé. Or because they bore a sense of obligation to their faith. I had trouble believing that any of these generous souls really, deeply wanted to help us.

I now know that such suspicions reveal more about who I was than who these people were. I recognize the irony: as a person of faith, I was supposed to believe in the inherent goodness of people. Yet it was difficult for me to conceive that a person would naturally and spontaneously, without being asked, bestow such an act of loving-kindness upon another in need, putting him- or herself out financially, emotionally, physically. If acts of loving-kindness were natural, I reasoned, everyone would perform them, not just a few. We wouldn't need theological and social mandates, such as the Biblical imperative "Clothe the naked, feed the hungry, support the widow and the orphan."

In my defense, my skepticism may have been the result of some of my experiences at the beginning of my career. Early in my rabbinate, I would appeal to congregants to do good for others—someone needs a ride to services, we need money for the roof, we need help with the youth group—just because these were the right things to do. Over the years, I discovered that people did not want to do things *just because*. They wanted to know, *What's in it for me? How will I benefit?* So I found I had to justify my appeals for help. I had to try to convince someone, saying, "This will be good for you, too." When asking for help on behalf of the community, I had to create another layer of meaning to make it more personally attractive and acceptable.

Over the years of Eyal's illness, as I pondered the acts of kindness that came pouring in, I kept looking to my faith tradition for insight. One core Jewish teaching holds that "the world is sustained by three pillars: the Torah, service of God, and acts of loving-kindness." That third pillar, acts of loving-kindness, used to puzzle me. In a text stingy with words, why the redundancy, *loving*-kindness? What does loving add to the kindness pillar?

It took a while, but I eventually came up with an answer. Left to our own devices, we tend to be self-centered and self-ish. Thus, we are reminded about what we must do to create a more gentle, generous, nurturing community. Acts of kindness on their own are not always from the heart; they often stem from obligation. However, once you introduce the descriptive word "loving," it is no longer about requirement or law. You don't perform acts of *loving*-kindness with an agenda or to fulfill a faith requirement. Loving is not thought of intellectually. It is visceral. There is no expectation of anything in return. When you perform an act of loving-kindness, you are not even aware you are doing it. The recipients are the ones who recognize it for what it is.

In 1998, Eyal was once again in the hospital, this time the Children's Hospital of Philadelphia. He was in his late teens, far older than most patients there. His blood sugar levels were dangerously high, he was in renal failure, and he was septic from an infection. Our four other kids were with us, and we were staying with relatives some fifteen minutes away by car. It was Christmas Eve. The hospital was quiet and only a skeleton staff was on duty.

Leah was planning to stay with Eyal overnight, while the

four kids and I were preparing to leave. The bell rang, signaling an end to visiting hours. "See you tomorrow, Leah," I said, kissing her on the forehead. She was already wrapped in a hospital-issued sheet and blanket on a narrow vinyl couch next to Eyal's bed. I brushed my hand across Eyal's forehead and gently pinched his cheek. "Nighty night, Eyal, don't let the bedbugs bite."

When I returned early the next morning, Christmas Day, Leah was excited. "You won't believe it, look at this!" She retrieved from the end of Eyal's bed an extra-extra-large bright green Philadelphia Eagles signed jersey, a compact disc player still in its packaging, and a large bottle of English Leather cologne. "Last night, I don't even remember what time, I was sleeping and I thought I saw someone come in the room. I figured it was a nurse checking Eyal's vitals. I went back to sleep. This morning, when I woke up, I was so surprised to find this. Before I could say anything to the nurse, she said to us, 'Santa Claus was here last night.' I told Eyal, 'It must have been Hanukkah Harry.'"

We later learned that all the children in the hospital had received gifts that night: teddy bears and coloring books and toy cars and dolls. The kindness demonstrated was remarkable. But I contend it was more than kindness shown to Eyal; it was *loving*-kindness. Somebody had taken the time to think to themselves, *This kid is seventeen years old. In many ways, he is a man. This is a children's hospital, and whereas the other kids revel in* Sesame Street *toys and Barbie dolls, this young man would appreciate something different.* The little bit of extra thought that went into choosing age-appropriate gifts for Eyal made that an act of *loving*-kindness.

• • •

Coming to really believe, understand, and appreciate the loving-kindness shown us was a turning point for me, prompting me to begin performing similar acts myself. I had always done acts of kindness; it is part of what I do for a living. Yet I did these nice things out of a sense of obligation. I got paid to visit people in hospitals. I got paid to make calls to those in mourning. I got paid to help people repair relationships. Over the years, having been the recipient of acts of loving-kindness many times over, I found myself naturally wanting to reciprocate. Of course, you can't always reciprocate to the one who delivered the "goods." So what do you do? You become part of the chain. You "pay it forward" by performing an act of loving-kindness for someone else.

The duPont Hospital for Children, in Wilmington, Delaware, sits nestled among the beautiful gardens and lush lawns of the former Alfred I. duPont estate. We had taken Eyal there on several occasions for extended inpatient "workups" and procedures. During one such visit in 1997, I met a cute little seven-year-old named Marty Baxter, or, as everybody referred to him, Baxter. He lived about two hundred miles from the hospital and was a frequent guest. He had a congenital orthopedic deformity that forced him to walk awkwardly, with clumsy braces. More often, he used a wheelchair. When I first got to know him, I asked, "Marty, when are you going home?"

He looked me square in the eye. "The doctors told me I'm going to go home when I can walk again."

Baxter was the unit's unofficial social director. Several times a day, he wheeled himself, uninvited and, frankly, unwanted, into another kid's room. Within a few moments, someone would say, "Not now, Marty, please come back later," and Baxter would leave, the door quickly closing behind him. Baxter may have been a pain in the tush, but if you scratched beneath the surface, you understood that in truth he was a very lonely boy who hungered for friendship and longed to be part of a caring community. Not once in all his weeks in the hospital did anyone visit this kid. Sometimes he talked about his mother and father. When he was ready to be discharged, they would be coming for him, he said. At seven years old, he had been left to heal on his own.

Even with our own sick kids and horrific challenges, many of us reached out to kids like Baxter, inviting them to be part of our community. When we went to the hospital gift shop, we always returned with two presents, one for our kids, one for Baxter. We made sure Baxter completed his daily menu requests correctly. We engaged him in conversation and advocated on his behalf.

"It's my birthday today," Baxter announced one day when he came into Eyal's room for his morning visit.

"Really?" I asked. "Well, happy birthday, big guy. How old are you?"

"Eight!"

I shook his hand heartily. "Time to get married, Marty."

He blushed and hung around the room a bit longer. He seemed a little down for a kid who was celebrating his birthday. A nurse came looking for him. "Marty, time for your physical therapy."

After he left, I turned to Leah. "I don't think Marty's having a birthday party. He never said anything about his parents coming."

I knew what I had to do. And I knew what I wanted to do. I went around to some of the other rooms where Baxter liked to hang out and invited the kids, their families, and a few nurses to a surprise party in the lounge after dinner. Later that evening, after the dinner trays were collected, I went to Baxter's room and said, "Marty, want to watch TV with me in the lounge?"

He brightened instantly. "Yeah."

I accompanied him as he made his way slowly down the hall with his metal braces. We entered the lounge, now decorated with blue streamers and balloons. The room exploded with a chorus of "Surprise! Happy Birthday, Marty!" On a table was a birthday cake with eight candles, munchies, lemonade, and presents. It was the only time during our many weeks at this hospital that I saw Marty Baxter speechless.

There's a piece of Jewish wisdom that suggests that the whole world is allowed to exist because of the deeds of thirty-six good people. It's a mystical story. These thirty-six do not know who they are, and neither do we. They are scattered and dispersed throughout the world. They are unassuming and modest and ask for nothing from those around them. Those who qualify for the thirty-six have a sixth sense that allows them to anticipate and respond correctly and completely to the legitimate needs of a friend, a neighbor, or even a stranger. Their sparks of goodness sustain and maintain a world in tremendous pain and conflict. The number thirty-six is symbolic. In Hebrew, the letters in the alphabet are assigned numerical values. The letters that make up the word for "*chai*," "life," add up to eighteen. Thirty-six is a multiple of eighteen, life.

I never thought performing an act of loving-kindness was something that anyone had a natural inclination for, but putting together a little birthday party for Marty Baxter felt so natural to me. Seeing his face light up at the sight of his friends in the unit and their parents was a tremendous gift— to *me*. There are moments when we have to work at being kind or generous. Maybe we feel tired, overwhelmed with our own problems. And there are other moments when we step effortlessly out of ourselves. We don't know where the energy and love come from. Those are the moments when we become part of that special community of thirty-six.

Connection

One night in 1986, not two weeks after Eyal's first, unsuccessful surgery to debulk the lesion, I was curled up on a couch in the parents' room adjoining the PICU, enjoying a bit of solitude, when I noticed an awful smell, rancid and sour. I tried to ignore the odor, but it persisted. Looking up, I discovered I was not alone. Tucked away in a corner, on another couch, was a couple in their early thirties. He wore overalls, a red and blue plaid shirt, mud-crusted duck boots, and a John Deere baseball cap. His disheveled hair was thick and black, his face darkened with three or four days of stubble. I assumed the woman next to him was his wife. She was tall and pretty, with light brown hair pulled back in a ponytail and no makeup. Judging from her body shape, she had recently given birth. She appeared drawn and exhausted, eyes closed tight, as she rested her head on her husband's shoulder.

The man and I locked eyes. Someone needed to speak, so I said hello and told him about Eyal. He told me he had driven in from Boonville, a small town about two hours away in the Adirondack Mountains. "Our baby got real sick the last couple of days. We don't have a hospital, so our doctor sent us here." He knocked on the wooden arm of his chair. "They say everything is going to be okay, knock on wood."

We continued chatting, and no longer just about our kids. "What do you do for work?" I asked.

"Pig farmer."

"Really? I've never met a pig farmer before."

He smiled. "Oh, yeah. You know, pigs get a bad rap. People think they're just good to go off to market and they're dirty. You know what? They are the most intelligent, clean animals around. I bring my pigs every year to the state fair here. Win awards, every single year. Sometimes I get so attached, I don't even want to sell them." I now understood the source of the odor. The man smelled as if he had come straight from the pigsty.

"So what do *you* do for a living?" he asked.

I hesitated, afraid of alienating or intimidating the pig farmer. In my tradition, a pig is bad news. Those who observe the Jewish dietary laws, even imperfectly, see pork as a religious and social taboo. A pig, or *hazier*, as we call it, is the embodiment of *treif*, forbidden food. But a hospital is no place for pretense and games. "Well," I said, "I'm a rabbi."

He shot me a look of surprise and bewilderment. Just as he was the first pig farmer I had ever met, I seemed to have been the first rabbi to ever cross his path.

At that moment, the farmer's wife lifted her head, opening her mouth in a small yawn. She whispered something to her husband and excused herself. "She's nursing," he explained to me after she left.

A few moments later, a nurse wearing a stethoscope stuck her head in the doorway. "Excuse me," she said, addressing the pig farmer, "is your wife around?"

"She'll be right back," he said. "She went to the milking stall."

I chuckled at his choice of words. I hadn't cracked a smile or laughed in weeks. It felt so good. It was such a necessary and wonderful release.

That five-minute exchange was the only conversation I ever had with the pig farmer. In the days and weeks that followed, I thought little of it; we were just two guys thrown together by circumstance, late at night, in a waiting room. It was a funny moment, a joke I could tell from the pulpit one day: "Did you hear the one about the rabbi and the pig farmer?"

But in the years since then, I've thought about him with some frequency. I realize now that our conversation called into question some of my most basic assumptions about other people. Although the pig farmer and I probably couldn't have been more different socially and religiously, the pain we each felt at seeing our child sick was the same. We were two fathers, sharing our stories, helping pass the time, trying to make sense of something that neither one of us thought we would ever have to face. Illness does not know *chochmas*—it does not make distinctions; it is arbitrary and random. To me, the pig farmer represented a larger, more important truth—one so simple and obvious that until I met him I had all but forgotten it: human beings are more alike than we are different.

Prior to Eyal's sickness, I had been incredibly insular. Judaism wasn't just a part of who I was, it was everything. I was raised in a Jewish neighborhood in Philadelphia and attended Jewish day schools through high school. My college of choice was Yeshiva College, a Jewish college, and then I attended rabbinical school. I dated only Jewish girls and met my wife at a Jewish camp. I never lived in an Orthodox or Hasidic community—I was exposed to the world, enjoying movies and sports and dressing like everyone else—but I retained a certain amount of skepticism and distance. American culture and Jewish tradition often clash—most notably on the Sabbath. While most non-Jews go out for dinner, shop, play golf, or enjoy other recreational activities on Friday night and Saturday, I follow Jewish law and observe the Sabbath. I don't drive my car, use the computer, or conduct any kind of financial transaction. Throughout my childhood, I found it hard to identify with communities outside my own, because my everyday life was so palpably different from others'.

When I grew up and became a rabbi, I remained devoted to my own faith community. I see now how self-centered, smug, and narrow-minded—not to mention haughty—I was. Despite my lower-middle-class upbringing, when I became a rabbi I no longer felt I had a great deal in common with the carpenters or shopkeepers of this world. In my mind, I had become an authority figure who hobnobbed with distinguished members of the congregation and determined what was permitted and what was forbidden for my community. The power was intoxicating, and it fed my ego. Deep down, I believed I had all life's answers and that the vast majority of people out there had little if anything to teach me.

I think back on that time and shake my head. How little I knew then. I know I am, perhaps, an extreme case, but certainly I was not alone in having distanced myself from those unlike me. Most of us do exactly that, in any number of ways. We lock our doors, buy burglar alarms, teach our kids not to talk to strangers, refrain from making eye contact on the subway, avoid cultural experiences that are not our own. We even keep our true feelings to ourselves, rarely sharing our innermost thoughts and never really connecting to others. When life overwhelms us, such isolation can become more intense. We retreat into protective cocoons, feeling besieged and misunderstood, pushing away those who reach out to us and extend a helping hand.

Yet disaster and heartbreak can also work in the opposite direction—if we let them. Because people of other backgrounds experience the very same traumas we do, and because sometimes offers of help and sources of strength and goodwill are found in the least likely places, times of pain and trauma can help to make us more open and connected than we ever thought possible. When this happens, the benefits are immense. Communing with a wider range of people, not just individuals who happen to be like us, we awaken to new experiences, insight, and contentment, even after our familiar worlds have been destroyed. We discover new parts of ourselves and put ourselves on a path to a renewed and unexpected wholeness. Little by little, we leave behind a part of our suffering and feel the contentment that comes with a more expansive sense of belonging.

How do we overcome our discomfort and experience connection to the fullest? We don't have to try very hard; it happens naturally and gradually. We just have to keep our eyes open to it. Think of my encounter with the pig farmer. I didn't have to wait long to be pulled again out of my neat little world. When Leah and I took Eyal to New York University Medical Center for his second high-risk surgery, we couldn't afford to fly him down ourselves. Luckily, we learned of an outfit called the Washington Aviation Ministry Medical Air Transportation Program (this was the original name of the organization; I believe today it is called something like Mercy Airlift). The ministry began as a volunteer air-transport organization for church workers and missionaries. It evolved into a medical air-transportation program serving the terminally ill, critical newborns, people who had been injured far from home, elderly patients who needed to be reunited with their families, and children like Eyal. Many of the pilots flew commercial airliners, and all of them were born-again Christians who volunteered their time, talent, and personal resources. They called themselves "Flying Samaritans" and saw themselves as "a group of Christians who feel [their] calling is to serve others, on a mission of mercy." When Leah and I had to transport Eyal from Syracuse to New York, the ministry came to our aid.

The plane, a yellow Cessna named *God's Wings*, bore a curious inscription on its tail: "Dedicated to the Lord's Service." On the day of the flight, the engines roared, and one of our pilots gave the customary preflight instructions and information. Then he added, "Hi, we are your pilots . . . We have twenty-nine hundred hours of flying time between us, and besides that, the Lord is with us . . . Rabbi, would you mind if we pray?"

Leah and I looked at each other in disbelief. Was this for real? A rabbi; a *rebbetzin*, or rabbi's wife; a little Jewish boy; two born-again Christian pilots; and an aircraft named *God's Wings*. For a moment, I felt uncomfortable. Born-agains, I had always thought, were out to proselytize. I was just waiting for their pitch. I had my dukes up. But the invitation to pray felt so spontaneous and sincere, and we needed some hand-holding. "I would like that very much," I said, with Leah nodding in agreement.

As the pilots prayed, I can't say I had a deep or meaningful religious experience. But I did feel a crumbling of my emotional walls. It didn't matter that these pilots believed that the Messiah had already come and I didn't. What mattered was that they were acting out of love and concern for a very sick child. These pilots were saying to me, *We care about you. We care about your wife. We care about your kid.* I would have never imagined, before Eyal got sick, that I would be praying with born-agains on a tarmac in upstate New York. But here I was, doing exactly that.

After we landed, Eyal was rushed from the aircraft to a waiting ambulance. My fellow parishioners, these "angels of the sky," offered us a closing benediction and sacred affirmation. "Rabbi, we will continue to pray for you, your family, your son." They approached the ambulance as Eyal's stretcher was placed into the vehicle. "God bless you, Eyal! God bless you!"

The surgery we had flown down for did not turn out as we had hoped. Eyal had his stroke and lapsed into his coma. We spent four excruciating, frustrating months at the hospital hoping, praying, that Eyal would wake up. It was during that time that I met Pedro. His department—"Environmental Services"—sounded official, but what it meant was that he spent eight hours a day pushing a mop, emptying wastepaper baskets, and scrubbing toilets. Pedro, a janitor from Mexico, modest and unpretentious, was at the bottom of the hospital hierarchy. But you would never have known it. He went about his tasks with a great, broad smile. He sang Spanish religious spirituals as he worked, his beautiful, rich tenor punctuated by a melodic whistle. In the PICU, Pedro was a local celebrity, and everybody awaited his appearance.

Almost every day, Pedro respectfully and considerately entered Eyal's cubicle. As Eyal lay motionless, Pedro mopped, cleaned, and asked Leah and me, "Do you need anything?" When he sang, I got the feeling he was serenading Eyal. Finishing his work, he pushed the bucket and mop into the hall and pulled the curtains closed to give us some privacy. A few seconds later, he poked his head back through the curtain. "So long, Eyal, see you tomorrow. Adios, amigo."

Before Eyal got sick, I never would have felt connected with a guy who mops floors. Yet I found myself looking forward to his visits. I welcomed his songs, his gentle presence. Pedro was part of the healing process for all of us. He conveyed goodness, strength, humanity—values that transcended my own imprisoning parochialism.

Pedro, the pilots, the pig farmer—these were just the first of many people outside my normal orbit with whom I would connect over thirty years as a result of Eyal's illness. Whereas at first I felt suspicious and judgmental, a lot of these people—parents, aides, nurses, receptionists, volunteers, therapists, custodians—showed themselves to be more open and welcoming than I could have ever imagined. They had no agenda, at least none that I could discern, and their openness and willingness to connect eventually wore off on me.

It is very hard to change a mind-set that has been fashioned since childhood. I don't know if I did it consciously, but over time I began enjoying conversations with people outside my comfort zone. I learned about birthdays and anniversaries, about the accomplishments of people in their families, about hobbies, favorite restaurants, family stories. Nothing was off-limits. I found myself extending myself and softening my own boundaries in ways I never could have predicted.

• • •

Jewish tradition says very little about how synagogues should look. Jews are commanded to erect an Ark to hold the sacred Torah Scrolls and to allow for an "Eternal Light" and windows. I can understand the need for the Ark and the Eternal Light—they derive from specific passages in the Bible. But why are Jews required to pray in a space with windows?

One interpretation I've heard is that windows beckon worshippers in by allowing in sunlight, the light symbolizing God's strength and warmth. That could be. There's no question that light pouring in through my synagogue windows always serves to remind me of God's presence. But maybe the windows are there not to direct our attention to what comes in, but to highlight the importance of keeping our gazes fixed outward. Windows enable us to look outside and see the needs of the greater community. Through a window, we can observe people we would never have looked at before and invite them into our lives. Windows in our spaces of worship and our homes prevent us from being insulated and isolated.

Shirley was a night nurse who worked for us during the early 1990s, when Eyal was in junior high school. She was a chubby, middle-aged woman with a terrific smile. She was also a drifter, a professional nursing migrant. A couple of years here, a couple of years there. Shirley did nothing in moderation. She was entertaining and cheerful but unfortunately not always reliable. Her choice of clothes revealed a "what the heck" attitude: she wore ill-fitting dresses, sometimes stained, with a slip two inches longer than the hem. Her car was a jalopy, more often than not in the shop for repairs. Although she was a single mom with an eleven-year-old son, in many ways she became Leah's and my sixth child. Her life was always in crisis, another calamity waiting to happen. But Shirley had a heart of gold; she would give you the shirt off her back.

Late one night in 1992, we were all snuggled in our beds. It had been a pretty uneventful day. Eyal had spent the day at school. The kids had done their homework, watched some television. Aroused from our sleep, Leah and I heard unusual noises downstairs. We exchanged looks and reassured each other that neither one of us had left on the radio or television. Yet the noise persisted. We were now convinced something was going on downstairs—nothing bad, not a burglar, but *something*. Leah gave me one of those wife-to-husband stares: *I worked hard today. I'm exhausted. The blanket really feels good. Chuck, please, crawl out of bed and check it out.*

I was not sure what awaited. I tiptoed down the steps, feeling conflicted: Did I really want to catch the culprit in the act? The strange sounds were coming from Eyal's bedroom. Peeking in, I found Shirley, a deeply religious woman and member of her church choir, standing at Eyal's bedside, eyes shut tight, swaying and rocking, humming and chanting, hitting a tambourine, singing a Christian spiritual with some unusual lyrics: "Jesus, this boy is going to walk again."

I made a hasty retreat to the bedroom, taking the steps two at a time. When I told Leah what I'd seen, she was speechless. We looked at each other in disbelief. We had never had a Christian prayer service in our home. In Jewish tradition, the home is sacred—a special, protected place. This was unthinkable. After a few moments, Leah sat up in bed. "What do we do?"

I did not answer right away. I knew what I would have done before Eyal got sick. But now, I had changed. I crawled into bed, pulled the covers up to my chin, and said to my wife, with a smile on my face, "Absolutely nothing."

Once one barrier falls, others begin to crumble, and we start asking ourselves: "Who am I?"

There is a Jewish story of a Reb Zusya, who had done everything good in his life. When Reb Zusya's time to die came, he was ushered before the Heavenly Tribunal, which would proclaim his status in the afterlife.

"Reb Zusya, why were you not Moses, our teacher?" he was asked.

"Because I am not Moses," he responded without hesitation. "I am Reb Zusya."

"Reb Zusya, why were you not Rabbi Akiba?" he was asked.

And again he replied, almost without hesitation, "Because I am Reb Zusya, not Rabbi Akiba."

This line of questioning continued, and Reb Zusya was compared again and again to great Jewish leaders, people of enormous accomplishment and great gentleness. Finally, he was asked, "Reb Zusya, why were you not Reb Zusya?"

There followed a long pause that seemed to go on forever. No answer. Total silence.

When Reb Zusya was compared to the giants in Jewish life, he had an easy fallback. He could dismiss those questions by suggesting that he was unique and that comparing himself to another was like comparing apples to oranges. But when he was asked, "Why were you not Reb Zusya?" he was essentially being asked, "Who are you, really? Were you true to yourself? Have you lived up to your potential?" This forced him to look deeply into his heart and soul. His silence, his lack of an answer, is the answer. He had no response because ultimately he didn't know who he was.

Before Eyal took sick, if I had been asked who I was, I would have danced around the question, spouting off superficial labels or titles. I would have said I was a rabbi, a Jew, a father, a son, a brother, a husband. Today, I know more deeply who I am. I am a person who has been tested, and who has survived. I am far less inclined to place myself above others, far more capable of learning from anyone, and far more willing to accept people on their own terms. I am, above all, a human being, imperfect and vulnerable like any other.

Over the years, as I started to let down my guard and connect to a wider spectrum of society, my professional life started expanding as well. Before Eyal took sick, I had not pursued many interfaith conversations. On those occasions when I engaged Christians or Muslims, it was out of obligation, but never because I had initiated those meetings or had any special interest in connecting with people of other faiths.

In the mid-1990s, I received a phone call from a Monsignor Joseph Champlin, rector of the Cathedral of the Immaculate Conception, the seat of the Bishop of the Syracuse Roman Catholic diocese. Father Champlin asked if he could come visit me in my study. I agreed, but I did not look forward to the meeting. I assumed that he wanted something from me—money or my participation on a charitable board.

It turned out that I liked Father Champlin; I found him self-effacing, soft-spoken, engaging, funny, and a terrific listener. Like me, he wasn't from Syracuse originally, and it turned out we had similar challenges—changing demographics, financial worries, institutions in decline. I also discovered that he was an accomplished and prolific writer, his books having sold more than twenty-five million copies. When I asked Father Champlin why he had come, he told me he had a dream: He wanted the two of us to exchange pulpits over the same weekend. He would speak at my synagogue on Saturday morning, and I would be the first rabbi invited to deliver the homily at his cathedral. Father Champlin asked me with such subtlety and kindness that before I knew it, I had put aside any lingering discomfort or inhibitions and was looking over the calendar to find a suitable date.

Father Champlin's appearance at our synagogue took place on a frigid January morning. Despite the weather, a large congregation had come for this unusual event: a priest addressing the synagogue. Father Champlin donned a black yarmulke, joking that he would have preferred a bright red one, like those worn by the cardinals, and I said, "Not yet, Father, maybe soon." Our service began at 9:15 A.M. and ran, as usual, for almost three hours. Father Champlin sat next to me the entire time, asking questions, making comments, trying to follow the Hebrew words. When he rose to speak, he remarked with a twinkle in his eye that after sitting next to me for three long hours, he now totally understood why so few Roman Catholics convert to Judaism. In this way, with genuine laughter and insight, he broke the ice, going on to speak not simply about building bridges between our communities but affirming our commonalities and respecting our differences.

The next morning, it was my turn. With its marble floor, stone walls, and high ceilings, the cathedral conveyed a remarkable feeling of awesomeness and holiness. Father Champlin beamed as he walked me around before the mass, describing the Biblical scenes depicted in the stained-glass windows. As I delivered my sermon, reflecting on how much I was growing as a clergyman and as a human being, just by virtue of being there, outside my comfort zone, I discovered through nods of agreement that many of Father Champlin's parishioners understood and related to the feelings of vulnerability I was describing. It occurred to me then that we are all in this together. And that mutuality warmed my heart.

Father Champlin and I kept in touch and became good friends; I called him "Joe," and he called me "Chuck." A year or so later, we began planning a trip to the Holy Land that would include people from each of our faith communities. We would first visit Rome for an audience with the Pope and walk through the Jewish ghetto there. Then we would travel to the Holy Land, admitting our differences, building on our strengths, learning from each other's histories and perspectives.

The trip never took place. First 9/11 happened, and then my friend Joe became sick with a blood disease that would eventually kill him. He spent his last months in service to others, writing, officiating at weddings, counseling families, and supporting his school for underprivileged kids. After he passed, I wrote an op-ed piece for the Syracuse newspaper that described this unusual relationship between a priest and a rabbi. I conveyed the mutual respect we had, our understanding that it was "kosher" to travel different highways to glimpse the top of the mountain.

Above all, I wrote about what I'd learned from Father Joe, including truths I had been assimilating since Eyal took sick. "I learned from my friend Joe that it's all right to be sad, it's all right as an adult man to cry and to miss a good friend. I learned the importance of community. I learned there are no shortcuts, and that all of us, at one time or another, must walk through the valley. I learned we are all survivors, and the criterion for friendship is just being there. And I learned there are lots of good people out there, not always from my faith community, and that you can become comfortable in each other's sacred space." Whereas before I had resisted connectedness, now I was preaching it loudly, proudly, and with reverence. It was that connectedness that was helping me to come into my own as a rabbi, and it felt great.

On Christmas Eve 2008, I went to the Jewish Home in Syracuse to visit my elderly parents. I brought my accordion, hoping to play some Jewish songs for them, accompanied by Leah, Eyal, and our other son, Erez, who is a great pianist. My mother had dementia, but she still recognized and acknowledged us. Old Jewish songs always evoked a smile from her; although she couldn't tell you what day it was or what she'd had for lunch, she remembered all the lyrics as she tapped her foot to the rhythm.

Erez and I wheeled my parents into an open area of the nursing home and began to play and sing. Within ten to fifteen minutes, we had attracted a large audience of residents, caregivers, and a few nurse's aides, Jewish and non-Jewish (despite its name, almost half the residents of the Jewish Home weren't Jewish). Some of the non-Jewish listeners wore Santa caps and Christmas pins. Remembering from my time in hospitals with Eyal how lonely it can be on the holidays, I turned to Erez with an idea. Somehow, he was thinking the same thing. Without exchanging a word, we turned from playing "Bei Mir Bistu Shein," a popular American Yiddish song, to offering renditions of "Jingle Bells," "Frosty the Snowman," and "Deck the Halls."

Years ago, I would have refused to play Christmas music. It just wasn't me. And if I had heard of a colleague who had done such a thing, I would have thought it inappropriate. But being the father of a sick kid had opened my eyes.

Eyal by this time had been wheeled into the room. There was my son, surrounded by a circle of elderly residents, everyone joining in song and celebration led by the rabbi and his other son, a soon-to-be-rabbi. We ended with a touching rendition of "Silent Night," followed by a rousing "Hava Nagillah," while my mother and father, of blessed memory, looked on and smiled.

Personhood

In September 1986, when Eyal had been in his vegetative coma for a couple of months, we passed the time and encouraged his recovery by talking to him incessantly about everything: Big Kenny (his buddy from nursery school), his favorite foods (Nanny's chicken soup and spaghetti and meatballs), sports, the weather. We sang his favorite song, the *Smurfs* theme song. We held photographs of his sisters and brother in front of his face. We got into bed with him and rubbed his back. But still he remained unresponsive, save the occasional involuntary tremor and an awful grinding of his molars.

Most of the medical staff who interacted with Eyal treated him at times in an impersonal way. They read the machines and paid attention to the numbers, sometimes forgetting that there was a little boy lying there. To them, Eyal was the stroke kid in the vegetative coma in room 11.

We understood: the staff needed to detach emotionally so as to do their work and survive in their very difficult jobs day after day. Still, it hurt. Leah and I instinctively countered by becoming fierce advocates for Eyal. We would remind the staff that even with all his machines, Eyal was still a real kid.

I will admit, the constant effort wore on us. I felt a powerful urge to escape the hospital and feel the sun on my face, even for just a few moments. I took frequent breaks, calling home five or six times a day to talk to my parents and see how our other kids were doing. I felt overwhelmed and powerless. There was nothing to do but push on day after day, attending to our son and hoping he would wake up.

One day, a woman whom I had not seen before entered the PICU. She was in her midfifties but seemed older. She was very proper, wearing a blue cardigan, a plaid skirt, and sensible black flat shoes. "Good morning," she said to Leah and me upon entering Eyal's cubicle. "I'm Mrs. Kravitz. I'm from the New York City school system. I'm the teacher assigned to NYU pediatric patients. School begins today."

Evidently the New York Board of Education was required to provide instruction to youngsters in a hospital environment, irrespective of the child's physical condition and intellectual capacity. This was not optional; it was a legislative mandate.

Mrs. Kravitz held a clipboard bearing Eyal's name and relevant information. Over her other shoulder hung a large canvas bag full of textbooks, workbooks, arts and crafts materials, administrative paperwork, and her lunch. Leah gazed sadly at the canvas bag, the markers and crayons. Eyal had always loved to draw.

"Eyal is in a coma," I told Mrs. Kravitz.

"I know that," she said kindly as she continued over to Eyal's bed. She pulled up a chair close to his head, took out a large storybook with lots of pictures, and introduced herself. "Hi, Eyal, I'm Mrs. Kravitz, your teacher. Let's get started."

In the ensuing days, Mrs. Kravitz came every morning at ten and stayed for an hour. She was incredibly focused.

Nothing deterred her. If an alarm went off signaling that Eyal's feeding tube had occluded, she knew how to silence it and reengage the feeding. She continued teaching even when the nurse entered to take Eyal's vitals, turn him side to side to minimize skin breakdowns, or suction out his breathing tube.

One day, perhaps a week or two after she had begun lessons, Mrs. Kravitz pulled from her canvas bag a timeworn Indian drum. After providing Eyal a brief explanation, she demonstrated how to use the drum, hitting it with the palm of her hand over and over again, for several minutes, in close proximity to Eyal's ear. Several nurses peeked in to see what the noise was all about.

I watched this interchange with admiration. A lot of folks had been ready to give up on Eyal, but not Mrs. Kravitz. She could have just as easily clocked in, sat there, and read the *New York Times*. Instead, she demonstrated fierce determination, loyalty, creativity, and passion—a respect for each person, regardless of circumstance or condition. She taught me a simple but powerful lesson: that each one of us, irrespective of where we are in life, who we are, and what we are capable of, deserves validation and attention. We deserve to be treated like human beings—people who *count*.

Heartbreak and loss test our notions of who has value as a human being. Is someone who can no longer drive, walk, talk, think, or breathe unassisted still valued? Does a person ever stop being a person and become a mere object, an "it"? Jewish theologian Martin Buber distinguished between what he called the "I-it" and the "I-thou." An I-it relationship is one that forms between human beings and inanimate objects like cars or televisions; an I–thou relationship is one between two living people with feelings and ideas, likes and dislikes. An I–thou relationship is special, a living bond rooted in mutual respect; the two parties make an effort to understand one another, educate one another, learn from one another. As Buber reminds us, we all too often confuse these two kinds of relationships, treating our objects as if they were people, and treating people as if they were mere objects—with dispassion, arrogance, and a lack of consideration.

To move ahead and achieve a new wholeness, we must redefine how we think of people, including ourselves. We must come to understand that we all retain human dignity *even if* we are no longer financially successful or married or healthy or revered by society. We are all athletes *even if* we don't run on two feet (but rather move a wheelchair down a track). We are all musicians *even if* we don't use our fingers to manipulate a piano keyboard (but rather our chins to control a computer program). At the extreme, we are all people worthy of consideration and basic respect *even if* we aren't able to think logically or express ourselves to others. As long as we possess a beating heart and an intact human soul, we're still unique human beings in the fullest sense and deserve to be treated as such.

The Bible tells us that we are created in the image of God. What does this mean? Do we actually have God's physical characteristics? Arms, legs, fingers, ears, eyes, nose? I don't think so. To me, this means that we all have that spark of the Divine within us. That spark remains even if we cannot feed ourselves, walk, turn our heads, or speak. By remembering that every person—no matter their health or circumstances—has a spark of the Divine within them, we recognize the essential humanity in each of us. We no longer disregard or write people off; rather, we open ourselves to the idea that *everyone* can soar and overcome seemingly insurmountable challenges.

As we broaden our notions of personhood, treating everyone around us in an I–thou kind of way, with attention, respect, and love, we become more content with our lives and more accepting of whatever misfortune has befallen us. We also become better people, more sensitive and empathetic, more in tune with our deepest humanity.

In February 1987, when Eyal was out of his coma and back in Syracuse but showing few signs of further recovery, many people in our community tried to help us by suggesting physicians they knew. Each doctor came with a long string of superlatives. *He is the very best. She is the preeminent specialist in her field. My brother-in-law swears by this guy. He is so good, you have to wait six years for an appointment. She wrote the book for that surgery. If I had to have that procedure, he is the only one I would use.*

On several occasions, we heard about a certain physician in Philadelphia, a Dr. Grindy, who was regarded as an authority on pediatric rehabilitation medicine. In my vulnerable state, feeling restless, impatient, and unsure about our present course of treatment, I was easily seduced by the notion that a single doctor could solve all of our problems. I took the bait. I called Dr. Grindy, and he graciously agreed to visit Eyal in his hospital room.

We scheduled an appointment for the last Wednesday in February. Dr. Grindy made it clear his time was very limited, so we arranged for him to come in the early morning and return home late that same afternoon. The day of his arrival,

I was very excited. Showing up early at the airport, I stood at the gate and scoured the arriving passengers, not knowing what Dr. Grindy looked like. Soon I spotted a tall man, thirties, blond, well dressed, in a black cashmere dress coat and red scarf, carrying a tan leather briefcase, clearly looking for someone to meet him. We made eye contact. "Dr. Grindy?" I asked.

"Yes," he said.

I put out my hand. "Rabbi Sherman—call me Chuck. Welcome to Syracuse. Thanks for coming. Here, let me take your briefcase."

Wanting to make the most of every minute with Dr. Grindy, I began the twenty-minute car ride to the hospital by offering additional background on Eyal. Dr. Grindy listened politely but did not ask questions. I stopped talking about Eyal and an awkward silence ensued. Wanting to fill it, I became more of a tour guide, pointing out the downtown, different hospitals, the Syracuse University Carrier Dome.

I had hoped Dr. Grindy would be outgoing and gregarious, someone more in the mold of a coach for the Notre Dame football team, a "rah-rah" kind of guy who would coach Eyal back to good health. Instead, he was soft-spoken and aloof. But I told myself I was probably being too quick to judge. Dr. Grindy had come with an impressive list of endorsements. I decided to give him a chance to work his magic.

We arrived at the hospital and took the elevator to the fourth floor. Opening Eyal's door, we found Leah and Eyal watching cartoons.

"Leah, this is Dr. Grindy," I said.

Leah stood up, smiled, and turned to Eyal. "Eyal," she said loudly, "this is Dr. Grindy. He came all the way from Philadelphia to see you. Maybe he knows one of the Phillies."

Dr. Grindy smiled, approached Eyal's bed, looked at him for several moments, but never said a word to him. He then got started, taking off his coat, placing it on the back of a chair, pulling out a yellow legal pad from his briefcase, and taking a medical history. We answered questions we had been asked hundreds of times already: Was it a full-term pregnancy? A normal birth? When did Eyal walk? When did he become sick?

The conversation lasted at most a half hour. Then Dr. Grindy stood up, thanked us for being so patient, and left the room without acknowledging Eyal. He set out to do the rest of his day's work: conferences with Eyal's nurses, several doctors, therapists. Dr. Grindy sat next to the charge nurse for hours, reading and rereading Eyal's charts, care plans, medical records.

At 4 P.M., Dr. Grindy knocked on Eyal's door. "We can talk now."

Leah and I walked to a small nearby conference room and sat down. Dr. Grindy flipped through his notes. "I've read the charts carefully and reviewed the medical records. I've met with many of Eyal's doctors, nurses, and therapists. I don't see any further recovery. With a serious stroke like this, after several months, what you see is what you get." He looked us both in the eye and adopted a tone of finality. "Eyal will never be able to come home."

I didn't know what to say. Dr. Grindy probably thought he was doing his job by being honest, but to us, his stark assessment felt brutal. He picked up his coat and put his papers back in his briefcase.

"Let me call a cab for you," I said, removing two twenties from my wallet. I was in no mood to drive him back to the airport. We shook hands. Leah did not look at him.

"I'll send you a written report in a couple of days," he said. And that was it for Dr. Grindy.

I couldn't fault him for his prognosis. He called it the way he saw it. What really stunned me was his process. Yes, Dr. Grindy had been meticulous; he asked the right questions, spoke to the appropriate people. But he had missed the most important person of all. He barely interacted with Eyal—he hadn't even glanced at him while taking the medical history. Nor had he once touched Eyal's hand, looked directly into his eyes, or attempted a conversation. The only information Dr. Grindy gathered had come through others. Eyal's personhood, his uniqueness, the fact there's no one else in the world like him, got lost in translation.

As angry as I was at Dr. Grindy, I had to admit that he reminded me a lot of myself—or the self I was before Eyal got sick. I had visited lots of sick people, some unresponsive or in a condition similar to Eyal's, and I had always felt uncomfortable. I engaged members of the family who were keeping vigil, but I never spoke directly to the person lying in the bed, convinced, as Dr. Grindy may have been, that it was an exercise in futility. I had accepted our society's notion that in the absence of a "quality of life," there is *no* life. I never pondered the basic question, Who gets to define "quality of life"? During my visits to the sick, I was in effect making a judgment call, pronouncing the person already gone.

But after Eyal got sick, I realized the gravity of my error. Who are we to determine that a person lying in a hospital bed doesn't hear a melody or feel a loving touch? Who are we to say that such a person is not comforted by the presence of family and friends or the words of a familiar prayer? I have seen many people interact with Eyal over the years, and I have learned that it is never an exercise in futility to talk with, sing to, pray with, or physically touch a person who is sick or compromised.

Today when I visit someone in the hospital, I approach the bedside almost immediately and engage that person in conversation. It doesn't matter if someone says, "Oh, she doesn't even know you're here." I will not be deterred. I sing and chant familiar prayers that even the most marginal Jew would remember from childhood. I talk to the person. I share with them common memories. I tell a little story. I let them know they are not alone.

I don't know if a sick person I visit is going to die today, tomorrow, or in ten years. I don't have that kind of power. But when family members see me treat their loved one with dignity and respect, when they see me projecting a sense of normalcy, when they see me recognize their loved one as a person who *deserves* attention, consideration, and care, they feel encouraged. Sometimes they begin to see their loved one differently, too. Whereas before the family might have ignored the sick person and referred to them in conversation as if they were not in the room, now they pay attention, sing the sick person a favorite song, touch their hair, hold up get-well cards. They work to create some kind of normal discourse under the most extraordinary and painful circumstances.

Leah, Eyal, and I have spent time in dozens of hospitals and clinics over the years. At the very best of them, the staff took the time to know Eyal. *Eyal,* they said, *would you like your head turned this way? Would you like the light on or off? Would you like the TV louder?* These kind and understanding souls knew that despite how grim Eyal's situation may have seemed, there was still life here. *All* life is important. Eyal was not just a broken body but a person with real preferences and needs.

Whether we're well or sick, we all have our own stories, our own unique fingerprints stamped in our hearts and souls, and we need others to affirm and validate our individuality. I have been in the presence of quite a few powerful public figures, and what has impressed me has been their ability, even in a large, crowded setting, to make me feel as if I am the most important person in that room. Imagine what might happen if *everyone* treated everyone else as worthy of attention, respect, and love. We'd see more genuine listening in our society, more understanding, more empathy, more connectedness, more tolerance of legitimate differences of opinion. We'd see far less of the conflict that comes when different communities not merely fail to interact with one another but lose sight of one another's common humanity.

Adam is the first human being in the Bible's creation story. Only later, because of Adam's loneliness, is Eve formed from his rib. Why does the world begin with only one person? Certainly God had the ability to create others. I think the Bible is communicating a message here about the preciousness of each one of us. At the time of creation, Adam represented the entire human race. If something happened to him, humanity was finished. And so it is, in a way, with all of us. There may be billions of us on this planet, but each person is invaluable, a world unto him- or herself. A rabbinic source says, "He who sustains the life of one person, it is as if he has sustained the entire world." The flip side: "He who destroys one person, it is as if he has destroyed the entire world."

• • •

How do we come to appreciate personhood more fully? We have to make a conscious and constant effort. With life moving so fast and so much technology distracting us, it's easy to sidestep our hearts and lose sight of others' humanity. We often don't stop to appreciate the uniqueness of each person we come across—the grocery store cashier who always smiles and asks how you are doing, the person in traffic who waves and allows you into the lane, the neighbor or family member who calls just to check in and say hello, without any agenda. It is exponentially harder to look beneath the surface and appreciate the distinct human presence of someone like Eyal, who relies on machines to breathe. Our family has affirmed Eyal's personhood to both ourselves and others by going to extraordinary lengths to give Eyal as much of a life as possible. Fighting battle after battle, we made sure he had a Bar Mitzvah like any other kid, and we have taken him to malls and amusement parks as well as on road trips to Boston, Philadelphia, New York City, and Atlantic City. Perhaps the most important thing we did was ensure that he received an education comparable to one that "normal" kids received.

Initially, we schooled Eyal at home, bringing in a teacher for an hour a day. Leah, who had trained as a teacher, read to Eyal, taught him math, and enlarged the newspaper so he could start reading part of it. In the late 1980s, we started sending Eyal to the local elementary school. At that time, society was in the early phases of changing the way it handled kids with physical and developmental challenges, taking them out of institutions and integrating them with other children. Our local school had been mainstreaming children with autism, and administrators were willing to consider taking Eyal. After many meetings, we came up with a plan. Eyal would go to the local elementary school for a few hours each day accompanied by his nurse and Leah, who could facilitate communication. The school district would provide an aide, and a teacher would continue to make at-home visits to supplement Eyal's education. The district would also take steps like instructing the other kids about who Eyal was and why he was there and providing a private room where Eyal could go to be suctioned and have his bags of waste disposed of.

From the beginning, Eyal loved school, soaking up knowledge and developing into an inquisitive, insightful, funny, and respectful child. The school environment became his community, his social network, just about everything. And yet, our experience wasn't entirely positive. We had to push hard for Eyal to receive respectful treatment from people who for one reason or another couldn't see him as a unique individual, a kid deserving of respect like any other. In junior high school, the gym teacher wanted Eyal to stay off to the side during floor-hockey games, concerned that he'd be injured. Leah would have none of that. She purchased a hockey stick for him, and the next day he sat in his chair, the stick attached, and moved up and down the gym floor, playing with the nurse. He wasn't part of the normal gym class, but at least he was included in some way. His personhood was recognized.

Perhaps because we fought so hard, Eyal has come to believe in himself, stay active, and develop a strong sense of individuality, leading others to notice that individuality, too. In middle school, a hall monitor whom he passed every day going into school saw him in the school chorus singing away (he would mouth the words, although no sound could come out). The next day she said, "Eyal, I didn't know you could sing." In his college Hebrew class, the teacher went around the room asking the students in Hebrew where they lived. Eyal answered, "*Rehov Sumsum*" (Sesame Street), surprising everyone with his sense of humor. Most people don't realize that Eyal knows what is happening in the world; in fact, he keeps up with current events and world news, knows a lot about sports, and even follows celebrities, thanks to his sister Orah, who reads *Us Weekly* and *People* magazine with him.

It's not just strangers and acquaintances who are taken aback by Eyal's engagement with the world. Even our family is constantly surprised to find that Eyal has opinions and desires of his own. We thought for his middle sister's Bat Mitzvah we would buy him a new pair of pants, a dress shirt, and a vest instead of a sports jacket, because a vest would be easier to put on him. But he saw that his brother was getting a nice new navy sports jacket, so he wanted one, too. No amount of reasoning with him could change his mind, so we walked out of the store with a navy sports jacket that looked just great on him. There was no question that he would wear a tux at both his sisters' weddings, which is why his own personal tuxedo hangs in his closet.

On other occasions, Eyal has startled us with his awareness of his condition and his sadness at what might have been. One night about two years into his college studies, Eyal mouthed to me, "I would not be going to Syracuse University except for my situation." What he was communicating was that he might have liked to go away to school like his siblings. Like anyone else, Eyal wanted to maximize whatever God-given talents he had, and he felt sad that this wasn't possible.

Over the years, having witnessed Eyal's growth firsthand, I have become an outspoken advocate for people with special needs. My chief task, I realize, is helping to broaden others' understanding of personhood. I remember a local city councilor who argued outrageously that we shouldn't spend money educating kids like Eyal, since they would never be productive members of society. At a public meeting, I pointed out that I've watched my son do things no one else could. It may have taken him a year and a half to move his thumb two centimeters, but that was just as important an accomplishment to him as achieving a PhD in nuclear physics may have been to someone else. It demonstrated every bit as much courage, determination, and strength. We are all individuals pursuing our own struggles as human beings, and we *all* need to be allowed and encouraged to become everything we were put on this planet to be.

Jewish law holds that a community requires at least ten people to hold a prayer service, or minyan. Traditionally, that meant gathering at least ten Jewish men, but nowadays more liberal synagogues follow the practice of gathering at least ten Jewish adults. Jews have an unusual way of counting individuals, especially for a minyan. Rather than simply assigning numbers to people—saying "One, two, three," etc.—the prayer leader typically counts using words. He or she recites a verse from the Book of Psalms, assigning a specific word of the verse to each person in the room. A favorite verse used for this purpose, comprised of exactly ten Hebrew words, is Psalm 28, verse 9: "*Hoshiyah et emekha evarekh et nachalatekha ur'em v'nasem ad haolam.*" "Deliver and bless your very own people; tend them and sustain them forever."

Why not count the usual way? Because people are not numbers. They are much more than that. Numbers are abstract, colorless, valueless. They are defined and finite. People are unique and individual and infinite. It diminishes someone to call him "three" or "seven" or "ten." During the

Holocaust, the Nazis reduced concentration-camp inmates to mere chattel precisely by revoking their given names, assigning them numbers, and tattooing these numbers on their arms. In Martin Buber's terms, they used numbers to reduce people to an "I–it" relationship.

Just as each word of a psalm contributes something unique and essential to the meaning of that psalm, so each person contributes something unique and essential to a community. A verse from a psalm would not be complete without each word, and a community would not be complete without each individual person. A verse is Divine, given to us by God. Bestowing a word from a verse onto individuals confirms that they have a touch of the Divine in them, that they are special.

The sight of Eyal today still makes many people uncomfortable. Yet he remains much more than the guy in a wheelchair who needs machines to breathe. He is and always will be our Eyal. He's someone who's living life. He has desires, dreams, and regrets. He feels joy and sadness. He has strengths and limitations, a unique way of seeing the world. He's constantly learning, growing, and changing. He's a person like you or me. A person who matters.

Communication

∞

By the week of Eyal's sixth birthday, fourteen months after that night in the blue bathroom, our family had settled into a routine. Leah kept Eyal company at the Syracuse hospital and saw to his needs. My parents, then in their early seventies, ran our household, doing the best they could to take care of thirteen-year-old Nogah, eleven-year-old Orah, four-year-old Erez, and our toddler, Nitza. I had returned to work: daily services, weddings, funerals, Bar and Bat Mitzvah preparation, teaching, pastoral visits, meetings. At every available opportunity, I made a mad dash to the hospital to relieve Leah. Most nights Leah slept at Eyal's bedside; occasionally I would fill in. The room was too small to accommodate a cot or recliner. We had to make do with a straight-backed chair, a pillow, and a thin mauve hospital blanket. Using an overturned trash can as a footstool, I was able to stretch out my long legs.

Eyal's quality of life was very limited. Although a teacher like Mrs. Kravitz came to teach him, her lessons only lasted an hour a day. The rest of the time, Eyal had little to do. Once in a while, a play therapist from the hospital appeared, but she was young and intimidated by Eyal's enormous physical challenges and deficits. The most she could do was tell us about the hospital's playroom and the books available for loan there.

Left to our own devices, Leah and I invented kid-friendly games and activities. Leah created an oversize deck of cards, coloring in the face cards and numbers, so Eyal could play Card Sharks, inspired by the popular television show, where you guessed whether the next playing card was higher or lower than the one before. I played the Name Game, over and over again. It went something like this:

"Eyal, baseball: the Philadelphia . . . ?"

He mouthed, "Phillies!"

"Eyal, a cartoon animal. Bugs . . . ?"

He mouthed, "Bunny!"

We never got bored playing the Name Game. Sports teams, cartoon characters, television commercials, names of nursery school classmates, aunts and uncles—you name it, I would get Eyal started and he'd guess what I was thinking, based on the clues I gave him.

One early afternoon, a few days before his birthday, I went to the hospital to relieve Leah. Eyal and I played the Name Game, continuing through his breathing treatment. I offered up a different kind of question. "Eyal, guess which aunt is coming to visit from Atlantic City this Sunday?"

Eyal's eyes lit up, and without hesitation, he mouthed, "Aunt Esther."

"You got it, big guy."

My aunt Esther, the second of my father's three older sisters, admitted to being seventy but was probably closer to eighty years old. She was as wide as she was tall, five feet across, and had been a widow as long as anybody could remember. Her hair color changed from week to week, depending on her particular mood and the color schemes available from the beautician. She was the original "Wandering Jew"; born in a small village in Poland, she emigrated to Philadelphia at the age of fifteen. Lacking the means to attend school, she worked as a seamstress and never learned to read or write. Despite life's disappointments and her frequent aches and pains, Aunt Esther remained the eternal optimist. She was cheerful, joyous, giggly; the phrase "shake, rattle, and roll" is a good description of an Aunt Esther chuckle. But what made her chuckle so remarkable—indeed, what made so much about Aunt Esther remarkable—was the fact that like Eyal, she had suffered a stroke. Her source of amusement had once been "schmoozing," the art of conversation. In a cruel irony, her stroke left her unimpaired except for an inability to articulate words and partake in what she enjoyed most: conversation, banter, and gossip.

The following Sunday morning, Leah and I met Aunt Esther, her son Carl, and her daughter-in-law Beverly in the fourth-floor waiting room. Aunt Esther wore a bright blue pantsuit with black flats, while her oversize pocketbook, tan artificial leather, was strapped tightly over her shoulder. In her other hand, she carried a stuffed frog with a long red tongue. You squeezed its belly and it said "ribbit." I gave her a hug and in return received a wet kiss on my cheek. Leah, too, received an Aunt Esther kiss. Pretty soon, Aunt Esther's heavy perfume had overwhelmed the strong, antiseptic hospital smell.

Eyal didn't usually have visitors except immediate family. Lots of people asked how he was doing, but very few actually came to see for themselves. Those who did visit felt uncomfortable; they often kept their coats on, beginning their visits with, "I can't stay long." But Aunt Esther was different. She positioned herself right at Eyal's bedside, and Eyal smiled wide. He didn't take his eyes off her, remembering our family trips to see this kind lady who laughed but made no sound.

Aunt Esther crouched over the bed, and she and Eyal continued to gaze at each other, just inches apart. She bent down, kissed his forehead, and rubbed her fingers along his face. A teardrop fell down Aunt Esther's cheek. Here were two people who were both unable to vocalize, but I could have sworn that room was filled with sound. Voices in passionate dialogue. A five-year-old and an eighty-year-old, chattering in an unconventional language, one more comprehensive and universal, a language of smiles and snickers, twinkles and glimmers.

I have to believe that Aunt Esther was telling my son, *Eyal, I know how you feel. Don't get discouraged. I love you.*

And he in turn was saying to her, *It's hard. I'm scared. But I'm trying.*

I am by nature loud and brash. I "do words" for a living, delivering sermons, eulogies, wedding addresses, Bar and Bat Mitzvah charges, lectures. I offer words of comfort. I am called upon to make toasts. I have always hated silent pauses, preferring the sounds of words spoken rather than quiet reflection. I have been told I dominate conversations and don't listen very well. In the wake of Aunt Esther's visit, I wondered whether words were quite as important as I had always thought. Maybe there was much more to listening than I had ever imagined. In yet one more area of my life, maybe there was a subtle source of value and wonder that I had never stopped to consider.

Most of us are far better at talking than we are at listening. When we do bring ourselves to listen, we pay attention to only one dimension of what we're hearing—the spoken words. As a result, we miss the nuances, and our lives and relationships become circumscribed and impoverished, without our even realizing it.

By committing ourselves to really listening, we find that new vistas open for us. We connect better with people. We become more sensitive and empathetic, appreciating others' personhood—even the personhood of people like Eyal who cannot express themselves in words. We become attuned to the nuances of what we ourselves might silently be saying. Learning to listen in the fullest possible way—aurally as well as intuitively—we move toward wholeness and peace, and we also recover some measure of the power snatched from us by heartbreak.

When the Israelites crossed into the Promised Land after forty years wandering in the desert, they arrived at the first entry point, the city of Jericho. This was hostile territory, and the Israelites needed somehow to get through the city's imposing walls. As recounted in the Bible, God told them: "Circle the walls seven times, to the sound of the blasts of the shofar, the ram's horn." The Israelites did that, and the walls crumbled. If we look at this story through a scientific lens, we can surmise that Jericho's walls may not have been that impressive, and that the vibrations from hundreds if not thousands of shofroth, rams' horns, might have conceivably caused those walls to come tumbling down. But another Jewish text, part of the High Holy Day liturgy, offers a different, less literal perspective. "The great shofar has sounded, a still small voice is heard." Shofroth can produce a variety of sounds, from explosive bursts to soft, gentle intonations. The second of these may seem less impressive, but they, too, are piercing and can bring down barriers. They bring down the *spiritual* walls between and within us. The message: Sheer volume isn't necessarily all-powerful. Softness and even silence have a power all their own.

Since Eyal took sick, I have learned that the conversations and interactions that stay with us most—that heal us, help us, and open our minds—are rarely introduced by the loud, shrill sounds of the shofar. More often than not, the connections that pierce the heart and soul resemble the still small voice: a wordless embrace, a spontaneous smile, eyes that look at us kindly—voices like those of my aunt Esther and my Eyal.

A Jewish story tells of a child in Eastern Europe who had come with his father to pray on the Holy Day of Yom Kippur. The community had filled the pews of the local synagogue, the congregants praying in unison, reading the sacred words. At first, the child said nothing; because of his limited education, he knew only two of the twenty-two letters in the Hebrew alphabet, *aleph* and *bet*, and felt intimidated. Some time into the service, the child began to whisper the only things he knew in Hebrew, "*aleph*" and "*bet*." He continued, his voice becoming louder and disruptive.

The people looked to the rabbi to quiet the young boy. The rabbi, absorbed in his own prayer, did nothing. Finally, a prominent member of the synagogue grew angry. Approaching the rabbi, he said, "Why don't you admonish the young boy? He is disturbing our prayers."

The rabbi lifted his head from his prayer book, stroked his beard, approached his lectern, and said to the congregation, "I understand there is a young boy here on this holy day who has been chanting the *aleph bet*. I admire his genuineness and intent. A lot of us say the right words without heart or understanding. '*Aleph bet*' is all this child knows. And that's all right. Because his words soar heavenward. And God, I am convinced, will fill in the rest."

We can show our concern for others with a minimum of words, or even none at all. From the pulpit, I see couples married forty, fifty, or sixty years reach out and hold each other's hands during services. I often don't know what prompts the gesture, but I realize that they are having a wordless conversation. You don't have to utter "I love you" to convey love. Sometimes just showing up can say so much to someone. People always remember who came to their father's funeral or sent them a birthday card.

Words sometimes limit our ability to convey raw emotion. A chuckle, a giggle, or a laugh communicates more than the statement "I am happy. I am overjoyed." A tear rolling down the cheek or a quivering lip says more than "I am sad." A furrowed brow conveys worry or anger more than the words "I am upset." A hug is sometimes the best way to say "I am your friend. I am here for you."

Since Eyal became sick, I have stopped making sure I have the last word. I have stopped rehearsing what I am going to say and become more comfortable with pregnant silences. Above all, I have become far more content just listening. I know that listening matters, that it makes a difference. Often people come to me and relate that they would go visit a friend or relative in the hospital, but they don't know what to say. I tell them, "Go and visit. Go and sit. The words aren't important. You don't even need to say anything. Just go."

• • •

How do we come to hear people who because of a disability have no choice but to speak very softly or in the absence of words? It's an ongoing challenge with no easy answers.

Today, my family communicates with Eyal by reading his lips. We looked into technology that would let him use his limited chin movements to activate a specially designed keyboard, which in turn would produce an artificial voice, but we rejected it, finding lipreading more natural. It's not perfect; most people outside our family find it too bothersome to read lips. When they visit, they don't ask Eyal what he thinks. I myself am not that good at reading Eyal's lips. Leah and our kids are much better at it, and even they find it tiring at times. When we try and try and still can't understand what Eyal is attempting to say, we get frustrated and so does he. Occasionally he'll give up, say, "Never mind," and retreat into himself. When this happens, we will often let the conversation go for the time being, not wanting to further frustrate him.

In general, though, Eyal has become quite adept at talking without words. When he lifts his eyebrows, we know something is bothering him. When he cracks a half smile, we know he is being mischievous. When he grinds his teeth, we know he is angry about something. When he blinks his eyes vigorously, he wants our immediate attention. When he shakes his head, we know the answer is no.

Listening to Eyal takes a great deal of effort. We have to look at his eyes and his mouth and concentrate wholly on him. We can't lose focus. If we deviate for an instant, let our eyes wander from his lips or pay attention to something else, we miss what he's saying. Over the years, I have come to see how this is a gift. Think of what might happen if we all communicated with each other in this attentive way. If we really and truly listened to our child who came home from school wanting to talk about gym or art class, rather than half-listening as we checked e-mail or pulled things out of the refrigerator for dinner. If we truly listened to our friends, without rehearsing in our mind what we were going to say in response. Think of how validated those around us might feel.

More often than not, people just want to be heard. They want someone to listen. They want someone to hear them. They are not looking for an answer. They are not looking for a response. Listening is a gift we can give one another.

Prayer is a lot like that. It would be great to know that God will act upon our prayers. But many of us pray simply in the knowledge that someone out there is listening. Certainly that is true in Judaism. During the Yom Kippur service, the congregation stands, the Ark is opened, and we all ask God together, "Hear our voices." Rabbi Edward Feld, the editor of the newest High Holy Day prayer book for Conservative Judaism, introduces this prayer with a startling thought about the centrality of listening: "As an owl in the desert screams in the night, so I want to be heard." In a spiritual sense, each of us is that owl. We are alone in the darkness, in the desert, confronted by existential realities beyond our control and our comprehension. We scream out, hoping that someone will hear us and help us to feel less alone. Consolation comes in the simple, primal act of being listened to.

To some extent, we can provide that consolation to ourselves. The Hebrew word for prayer, "*l'hitpalel*," is a reflexive verb, suggesting that prayer is not just intended to be heard by God but by *oneself*. By listening to ourselves pray, we can clarify who we are, what we want, and what challenges we face. Our real, inner selves are so often drowned out by others' voices or by the noise and distractions of everyday life. By learning to hear our inner voices, we become more whole and comfortable in our own skin. The owl's scream diminishes.

Eyal has taught me that people can find new and creative ways to make themselves heard even in the absence or near-absence of spoken language. When he got sick, Leah, who had majored in design in college, devised a mouth stick with a paintbrush for him to use. Eyal had always enjoyed working with his hands as a small child: Play-Doh, coloring, finger paints, chalk on the driveway, jigsaw puzzles. Leah figured that painting might be a nice way for him to pass the time and a good way for him to express himself.

Eyal started painting with Leah holding the palette and heavy paper. Given his very limited ability to control or support his head, painting seemed incredibly difficult and time-consuming, yet Eyal took to it. Soon, he wanted to paint objects that were in his room or visible through his window. He painted objects from the Bible stories I read to him, like Joseph's coat of many colors, or skyscrapers he had seen in magazines. He especially loved to paint flowers and found that he was really good at it. Painting validated him. Despite all that he had been through and the toll it took on his body, he could still create something.

Some months after Eyal started painting, I went to the mall and bought him a navy blue French beret and designer sunglasses. I started calling him "Pierre the Artist." He didn't like it. He would "say" to me, raising his eyebrows, *Take that stupid hat off my head.* Eyal's artwork was how he expressed who he was and what he thought about life. He didn't want to be turned into a stereotype. I remember in particular a beautiful painting he had worked on for weeks, a bouquet of lovely red roses that Eyal and the other kids had given Leah for Mother's Day. He called the finished work *Stem Gems*. I once asked him, "Eyal, why do you paint flowers?" He thought for a few moments and said, mouthing his words carefully and thoughtfully, "Because you have them forever." It was a strange answer. Eyal was bright enough to know that flowers wither and die. What was he really trying to say? I thought about it many times over the years, and now I believe that in a way Eyal was right; you do have flowers forever. You have the fragrance, the scent, the memory. There is something beyond the physical about a gorgeous flower that always stays with you.

My daughter-in-law, Rabbi Nicole Guzik, recently led a group of ninth graders on a trip to Israel. While there, the group toured a conceptual art exhibition called *Dialogue in the Dark*, in which participants made their way through a maze of rooms in total darkness. No exit lights, no windows—not even light from cell phone screens was allowed.

Before entering the exhibit, the group learned that their guide through the rooms would be a blind man named Saadia. Nicole was initially apprehensive. How could a blind man safely lead a group of twelve through hallways, up stairways, around bends, and between obstacles in pitch darkness? It seemed impossible. Yet she made a conscious decision to trust that this stranger would help them find their way, despite his disability.

Members of her group began to walk through the darkness and immediately they stumbled and knocked into one another. Saadia cleared his throat and whispered, "Stop. Before we begin, you are going to have to learn how to listen.

Let's start by having each of you tell me your name." They did so and continued on the tour. To help comfort Nicole, Saadia constantly repeated, "Nicole, are you there? Nicole, are you with me?" My daughter-in-law answered, "Saadia, I am here. I am with you." Despite standing in a room in which her sight was impaired, she was no longer afraid. A blind man was teaching her how to listen. A blind man was teaching her how to trust.

After the tour, Saadia led the group into a dimly lit room. Seeing Saadia for the first time, Nicole found him exactly as she had imagined: a small, older man with a warm smile. He gathered the group around him. "I am going to ask you to listen one more time. All my life, people told me that because I was blind, I couldn't aspire to greatness. I am a father, a grandfather, and a doctor . . . I am a busy man. Never let what other people say about you hold you back. Never let those opinions transform into your own. One could have seen my loss of sight as a tragedy. Instead, I looked at the gifts God bestowed upon me and realized, there is so much I can offer this world."

Nicole and members of her group all agreed that in the dark, their first inclination had been to grope the walls and try to find their way. Saadia had taught them that when we are living through a dark moment in our lives, often the best way to find light is to stop for a moment and listen to what the world is really trying to tell us. We need to stop the chatter in our heads and allow ourselves to trust what the world provides.

When Adam was in the Garden of Eden, he started to become afraid as the primordial light began to fade. He felt lost, alone, cold, and scared. Just as his fright was becoming too much to endure, he heard clinking at his feet. Taking a deep breath, he looked down. Two pieces of flint. Adam smiled and took the stones, struck them once, and created a fire. At the loneliest moments of our existence, when we take a moment to breathe, quiet the voices of paralyzing terror, and truly listen, we discover the gifts that God has already bestowed. Complete listening means having faith in our abilities and trusting that God will provide the rest.

Eyal's Bar Mitzvah year was difficult for me. Jewish tradition expects boys to declare their Jewish manhood in front of the community upon turning thirteen. Words figure centrally; by publicly reciting the Torah portion and openly declaring his place in the community, a boy celebrates his entry into Jewish adulthood. All that year, I found myself officiating at the Bar/Bat Mitzvah ceremonies of Eyal's old nursery school friends, with party celebrations held in the synagogue ballroom. It was hard to watch kids Eyal's age running around, lining up for cake, dancing, doing the limbo.

What made it tolerable was knowing that Eyal, too, would have a Bar Mitzvah, albeit in his own unique way. We had started him two years earlier on the standard Bar/Bat Mitzvah training, teaching him Hebrew; schooling him in basic prayers, history, and rituals; and showing him how to chant from the Torah scrolls. Since Eyal couldn't vocalize, we had had to teach him to open his mouth wide and use exaggerated lip movements so that those around him could see him articulating the words as they might normally be chanted. It was going to take an enormous effort to be understood by members of the congregation who had never read lips before and who, in some cases, weren't that fluent in Hebrew.

We had also thought a great deal about the logistics of

the service. Our pulpit is ten steps above the congregation, totally inaccessible for people in walkers or wheelchairs. To get around this issue, the congregation agreed to build a ramp that anyone with mobility issues could use going forward. A trickier problem was the sheer size of our sanctuary—how would people throughout the space be able to see Eyal mouth his words? We thought of projecting images of Eyal onto a giant screen, but that posed problems of its own. Jewish law forbids the use of electricity on the Sabbath; our fairly traditional congregation had used microphones and sound amplification equipment, but never the kind of sophisticated video equipment, including cameras, large screens, and wiring, that we would now require. If we allowed it on this occasion, we risked setting a precedent for the future that would, over time, degrade our adherence to the traditions we held dear.

As rabbi, I was the *mara d'atra*, the authority, so I could make final decisions about our congregation's religious practices. The questions about precedent troubled me, and I also knew that if I allowed the new technology I would face criticism from members who thought I was bending the rules for my family. To make a proper decision, I removed Eyal from the equation and asked myself: How would I respond to another family who had a child like Eyal? What would I tell another family in search of community? I knew what my heart and soul were telling me. My child, any child, who wants a Bar or Bat Mitzvah deserves to have one, and we should do whatever it took to allow that to happen.

I remembered a conversation I had had with my father many years earlier, when just beginning rabbinical school. My father was a junk dealer who had finished school in the ninth grade. While we were talking, he referred to a medieval Jewish text called the *Shulchan Aruch*, which most rabbis study as part of their training. "You are a pretty bright kid, Chuck. I am proud of you. If I had the opportunity for an education, my life might have been different. I would have wanted to be a rabbi. But wherever your life takes you, please remember this. Most people think the *Shulchan Aruch* has four books to it, right?"

I nodded yes.

"Well, you might be surprised to know there's a fifth book that nobody has ever heard of."

I smiled at my father, thinking he was teasing me.

His face tightened in seriousness. "Chuck, that fifth book is the most important book when it comes to living your life and making decisions according to Judaism. And that book is the book of *seichel*, the book of common sense."

When it came to Eyal's decision, common sense told me to be more flexible with Jewish law than I might otherwise have been. I ruled that the synagogue would allow the video recorder and television screens. My reasoning: it was comparable to the microphones we already used in that it served to "amplify" Eyal's only means of communication, the movement of his lips.

On Saturday morning, June 11, 1994, every last seat in our sanctuary was filled fifteen minutes before the service was to begin—over a thousand people in total. Another five hundred guests crowded the aisles. Even the unwritten Jewish eleventh commandment, "Thou shall not sit up close to the rabbi and cantor," was discarded and rejected. The closer the better: everyone knew they were going to witness something rare and miraculous.

A thirty-foot-wide movie screen had been set up on the pulpit. It dominated and obscured almost everything else, including the large Ark containing the Torah scrolls, several mahogany lecterns, and eight brown upholstered chairs for clergy and honored guests. Directly behind the screen, we had built a platform to position a rear-view projector. Several large television sets were scattered about the sanctuary. Three state-of-the-art television cameras were ready to roll, each placed to provide the greatest exposure. Cables, cords, and thick black extension lines ran throughout the building to several large mobile production-unit trucks parked on the synagogue's front lawn, all of this provided by a generous member of our congregation. With everyone assembled, Eyal sat up front, in the aisle, the only space that would accommodate his very large wheelchair. Leah sat next to him, and our other kids filled up the first pew.

From the pulpit, I pronounced the traditional invitation: "Rise and stand, Eyal David, son of Rabbi and Leah." Similar words have been said for centuries. I wouldn't change them for Eyal, even though he couldn't stand on his own. Leah stood up, positioned herself behind Eyal, and pushed his wheelchair up the recently installed ramp in the sanctuary's right-hand corner. For the next few hours, Eyal, dependent on his ventilator for each breath, silently mouthed the standard Hebrew blessings, the Maftir and Haftorah, and led the liturgy.

Midway through the service, it came time for Eyal to deliver the *d'var* Torah, a personal reflection related to that morning's scripture reading that usually lasts five to ten minutes. It had taken weeks, but Eyal had typed out this speech himself using his computer and mouth stick. In front of the hundreds gathered that day, Eyal said, "Even though my Bar Mitzvah is different or awesome, or radical, being high-tech, I never thought about that. I just always knew that when I reached age thirteen, I would be here on the *bimah* [pulpit] and have a Bar Mitzvah, just like any other kid."

The unexpected and sustained applause that greeted these few words confirmed that Eyal had taken his place among our community as a man. But he had accomplished still more that day. He had given our community a gift of hope and resiliency. In his own language, using his silent "spoken" words, he had sent a strong, unforgettable message: that nothing, absolutely nothing, was impossible.

Like my aunt Esther, Eyal had spoken with the "still small voice" of the shofar, and what he said resonated more deeply and powerfully than any ordinary words I or anybody else could have uttered.

Marriage

∞

Most Saturday nights, Leah and I go out for an hour or two, just the two of us. Saturdays, the Jewish Sabbath, are the most difficult day of the week for her. It's hard to find nurses to help Eyal during the day, and I am at synagogue officiating at services, so Leah handles Eyal's nursing care herself, in addition to what she usually does as a mother—listening to him, entertaining him, reading to him. It's a tall order, but Leah accepts it graciously. No resentment or complaints from her.

And yet, we all have our breaking point. One Saturday evening, after a nurse had come to relieve Leah, we prepared to go out for pizza. The wind was blowing and snow was falling. I had forgotten to pull the car into the garage the day before, so the inside was freezing and a layer of ice and snow crusted the windshield. We got into the car, and I turned on the ignition, blasted the defroster, and sat there waiting until the smallest of circles had cleared on the windshield. I should have gotten out to scrape the windshield myself, but I didn't want to—it was too cold.

Leah shivered beside me. "Aren't you going to turn the wipers on?"

"Leah," I said, "they're frozen. I have to wait."

Finding a couple of tissues from her coat pocket, she tried to rub the inside of the windshield.

"Leah," I said, "there's a brush and scraper in the backseat."

She smiled. "Good, it will take you five seconds."

"I don't have my boots on," I protested.

Finally, in a huff, Leah got out, opened the back door, and took out the brush and scraper. She walked to the front of the car and within a few seconds had cleaned the entire windshield and dusted off the headlights. She reopened the back door, threw the brush and scraper down on the floor, and slammed the door shut. Throwing herself back into the front seat, she yelled, "This is freaking ridiculous!"

We sat there for a moment. And then we broke out laughing. She was absolutely right. I was being ridiculous—selfish, inconsiderate, and small-minded. She had already given so much that day—I couldn't get out to clean the windshield? On a deeper level, everything we had been through these past thirty years had been ridiculous—unexpected, absurd, unbelievable. We have found over the years that humor can redeem so much in life, especially when it is shared. We weren't perfect as a couple, but then again, what couple is? I apologized to Leah and let her know how much I appreciated and loved her. The two of us continued to laugh together for the rest of the night.

I first saw Leah on a Saturday afternoon in late June 1969 at Camp Ramah in the Poconos. I was twenty-three years old and in rabbinical school; she was eighteen and had just completed her first year of college. I was head sports counselor at the camp; six feet tall; thick, dark brown hair; terrific tan. I drove a two-seat green Triumph Spitfire and regarded myself as a BMOC—Big Man on Campgrounds.

On Saturdays, camp tradition called for religious services in the morning followed by lunch, the best meal of the week, and then a staff softball game. That Saturday afternoon was staff orientation week, so campers had not yet arrived. I was pitching for my team, the perfect position for me to see and be seen. I had attended this camp for ten years. I knew everybody, and I guess everybody knew me. I was somewhat surprised to spot a very pretty young girl, new to the camp, sitting under a tree down the third-base line.

Leah was wearing a faded blue work shirt and cutoff jean shorts. Her hair was straight and dark brown with gorgeous red highlights and bangs that almost reached her eyes. Her skin, even at a distance from the pitcher's mound, was like a china doll's, while her glasses were the old-fashioned, wire-rimmed "granny" type. She, too, had come to the baseball field to see and be seen, but she was a little more circumspect. She brought a book by e. e. cummings, and periodically she lifted her head ever so gently to watch me pitch.

Leah has always had an air of gentleness and goodness about her. Some misunderstand her; because she is so quiet, they think her distant and aloof. Those who know her realize that it's more timidity and shyness. In any case, I found her innocence so refreshing. She had no pretense, no affectation, no need for games or competition.

That night at dinner, I made sure I sat at this new girl's table. She seemed a little intimidated that the head sports counselor was paying attention to her. I learned that she was from Philadelphia, was active in her synagogue youth group, and had come to camp to serve as an educator's assistant.

As much as I thought Leah was interested in me, she didn't seem impressed by some of my pickup lines, or my fancy car, or the fact that I was in rabbinical school. Toward the end of the meal, I asked if she wanted to go out on a date that night after we had completed our camp responsibilities. She agreed. We became a couple that summer and were married a year later, in October 1970.

Today, after forty-three years together, our relationship is as strong as ever. We are, as always, each other's best friend. While illness, death, business failure, infidelity, addiction, depression, general unhappiness, and other difficulties often strain marriages to their breaking points, our bond has served as a source of strength, enabling both of us to build a fulfilling life for our family even while facing the realities of Eyal's condition.

Why hasn't our marriage crumbled? I have been asked this many times. I used to evade this question, regarding it as motivated by nosiness or fascination with somebody else's marriage. Over time, I have come to think differently. What people are really wondering is, "Could *my* marriage or my relationship survive such a test?" People look at the problems their own relationships face, which are seemingly not as acute as ours, and they ask, "How do the Shermans do it?" How can a couple jointly carry the broken and the whole?

Before Eyal took sick, if you had asked me the secret to a happy, enduring marriage, I might have answered by presenting a litany of "must-have" items. Top of the list: unconditional love. If you have to convince yourself to marry someone, if you have to do an advantages/disadvantages assessment, you probably should forget about it.

Second, I would have listed commitment to the marriage itself. The Talmud says that a wife's burning of the food is sufficient grounds for divorce. I think what the text means to say is that if something as small as burning dinner makes one ready to divorce, the wife is better off without her husband, as he has no commitment to her or the marriage.

Third, trust and honest communication. Keeping your partner in the dark about your feelings and actions can torpedo a marriage.

Fourth, there needs to be more happiness than not. If every day is a chore, then the marriage is already in the process of disintegrating.

Fifth, luck. So much in life is random, beyond our control. You just have to hope and be lucky.

I still believe in all of the elements on my original list, but after so many years, so many shared joys, and so many periods of irritation and conflict, I would add another item as well: an almost limitless willingness to give of yourself. Like it or not, you have to have that in order to carry the broken and the whole together as a couple. As the Bible suggests, and as our own experience confirms, willingness to give is the very definition of love itself.

Leah and I only survived these past thirty years because we depended on one another to give and keep giving. When I was down, she lifted me up. When she was down, I lifted her up. When Eyal was down, we both lifted him up. Neither Leah nor I ever gave a thought to walking away from our marriage any more than we would have considered abandoning Eyal. Over the years, Eyal's illness has allowed us to understand the essence of what a marriage is all about. It's not about merely enjoying each other's company, or being lovers, or being best friends. It's about being partners in giving. It's about reaching out as one united front to others so as to make their lives better. And at the end of another long, exhausting, painful day, it's about lying in bed together, holding hands, and saying, "Yeah, we did good today."

Leah and I have certainly experienced our share of tensions as a result of Eyal's difficulties. This was especially true during the late 1980s, when Eyal first became ill. With all the frustration, fear, sadness, and guilt we felt, normal, everyday bickering often intensified, escalating into real fights. Our greatest source of disagreement concerned how to handle Eyal's care. Leah was more trusting of doctors than I was. This gap between us increased after I began to take a critical eye and research Eyal's care more exhaustively. We often disagreed, and on such occasions she would roll her eyes in disapproval or speak to me curtly. Sometimes she got angry, and legitimately so, when she felt I was dismissing her opinions too quickly.

Despite all of the tensions, we always managed to take a step back and look at our situation from a broader perspective, to prevent ourselves from getting lost in the trivialities. There was no denying that we experienced tears, shouting, and periods of silence. But we both understood that we had a greater, joint task to face up to, and we were not going to be able to do that by ourselves. We both wanted what was best for Eyal and our other kids, and in the end, we determined that we would not allow our egos to get in the way.

Our most difficult period came in 1986, after Eyal's first surgery and before we took him to New York City. The doctors allowed us to take him back home with us for a couple of weeks. He looked like the Pillsbury Doughboy, pumped up on steroids to reduce swelling around his brain stem. He had a trache to give him a better airway, his gait was very unsteady, and he was irritable, crying much of the time. The pressure was enormous. Someone had to be with him at all times. If he gasped for breath, Leah or I had to rush over to him and examine his body from head to toe, looking for anything unusual that would signal a medical emergency. We took his temperature almost hourly. We felt his pulse. And at nighttime, Leah or I stayed in bed with him, listening to the beeps of the apnea monitor, leaving our hands on his chest to make sure he was breathing.

We had insisted on radiation therapy, even though the doctors had told us it wouldn't do any good. It at least gave us the satisfaction of doing *something*. Each morning, we dressed Eyal, lifted him into the backseat of the station wagon, and schlepped him to the hospital for fifteen-minute treatments on his brain. We had three other young children who needed to be fed, cleaned up after, and taken to school. Leah was seven months pregnant. Our house was out of control—dishes in the sink, laundry piled up. It was nearly impossible for us to keep our normal lives going.

One night, we reached a breaking point. Leah decided she wanted to give Eyal a bath. Even before he got sick, Eyal had resisted baths, lying on the bathroom floor and screaming. This time, although he was sick, he still managed to put up a fight. I don't know where his energy came from, but he was like a caged tiger, making it hard to even pull off his pajama shirt. I gave up the fight. "Leah, it's only a stupid bath. Let's just try again tomorrow. He's already got enough to deal with. Why add this?"

Leah kept trying to remove his clothing. "He'll feel better once we've done it. The warm water will calm him down."

I argued my case, but she would have none of it. That's the thing about Leah: once she makes a decision, she's immovable.

We got Eyal into the tub and began bathing him. After

a few minutes, he closed his eyes, stopped crying, held his breath, and started to turn blue. That did it. "Leah, look what you've done. He's dying!"

"He's not dying."

I screamed loud enough for the whole house to hear. "Yes, he is. Look what you did to him. Couldn't you just leave it alone?"

It got uglier from here. Leah was kneeling next to the tub, two arms holding Eyal, clothes wet. I stood towering over her, not bending down to help. I threw a bath towel at her. "Leah, this can't go on like this. Forget the damn bath. Get him out!"

Lacking the strength to fight back, she started to cry. "What do you want from me?" She pulled Eyal from the tub, cradling him in her arms.

We carried Eyal back to his room. Leah lay down next to him and rubbed his back, still crying. I walked out of the room to pull myself together. The other kids were standing around, all crying as well. It was an extraordinarily painful moment. I knew that I had meant my words to hurt.

Later that evening, I apologized for being so cruel. Leah admitted that the bath wasn't such a great idea. And like that, we moved on.

So much guilt. So much pressure. And that horrible uncertainty about what would happen to Eyal and our family. It all just took its toll that night. But we pulled through— something we would find ourselves doing again and again, without at the time understanding how.

The first mention of love in the Bible comes in connection with the patriarch Abraham, in a story that often strikes contemporary readers as disturbing and even incomprehensible. God and Abraham have developed a wonderful relationship, yet it appears God is not convinced of Abraham's loyalty. God devises a test, commanding Abraham to take his beloved son, Isaac, to Mount Moriah and sacrifice him. God demands, "Take your son, your only son, Isaac, whom you love . . . and sacrifice him as a burnt offering." Will Abraham do it? The answer is yes. Abraham is about to act on God's command, performing the ultimate sacrifice by offering his son Isaac, when an angel calls out, "Stop!" Abraham passed the test.

According to Rabbi David Wolpe, God's commandment that Abraham offer Isaac, whom he loves, teaches us that "all love has an element of sacrifice. The Hebrew word for sacrifice, *korban,* comes from the root 'to draw close.' When you sacrifice for another, it seems, you draw close to them—an idea encountered elsewhere in Jewish tradition, too. Jewish law holds that in order to become engaged to someone, one must offer a gift. All relationships require a willingness to give; to love another as friend, family, partner, you must make an offering of yourself. When we in modern-day America ask whether someone is in love, we often ask, 'What do you feel?' We might better ask, 'What would you give?'"

When I think back on all Leah has given to our family, I find myself amazed. This once-shy, quiet woman has demonstrated seemingly limitless strength and determination. She never complains about her lot in life and pushes all of us to do our best rather than wallow in self-pity. Enjoy the little pleasures in life, she says. Stay engaged and active. She is able to see joy where others would see only distress. She has never said to any of our kids, "I don't have time for this now." And even today, they rely upon her wisdom, intelligence, and judgment.

I asked Leah to reflect on our marriage and on what she thinks she's given me. She said, "I never felt that our marriage would fall apart because of Eyal's situation. Of course we had arguments and fights, but who doesn't? I always wanted a large family and I realized that there is responsibility that comes along with it. One goes into a marriage with the intent to stay married. Just because something doesn't go as planned doesn't give us the okay to walk out." Leah also shared with me a memory. Early in our marriage, before we had any children, we were having an argument about something trivial. Her father, who was present at the time, turned to Leah, looked her square in the face, and said, "Just put up with Chuck's craziness." Leah's father realized that our quarrels weren't serious and that she was going to have to decide to just live with my imperfections. These words really stayed with her. From then on, whenever something I did irritated her, she would think of her father's advice.

It's true: we sometimes struggle in our relationships until we realize that what we are called to do as partners and lovers is give of ourselves. One couple in my community raised a son with profound physical and emotional challenges, as well as two healthy children who grew into accomplished adults. Some years after the son was diagnosed, overwhelmed with the daily grind, the wife became despondent to the point where she could not pull herself out of bed. This woman had always been full of energy, yet now she took no interest in anything. All she wanted to do was sleep.

The husband was concerned, but at first he decided to ride it out, thinking it was just a phase his wife was going through. Finally, frightened for his wife's health, he called his mother-in-law in Baltimore, who immediately came to try to cheer his wife up. Even this didn't help.

One day, the woman went downstairs to get something to eat. Walking into the kitchen, she saw that the sink was over-flowing with dirty dishes, open cereal boxes were crowding the table, cabinets were half-opened, and several pizza boxes had been stuffed into the trash compactor. The wife stood there for a long time, surveying this utter mess. And, as she tells it, something changed in her. Something happened. It hit her right then, standing over a sink, that her family needed her to keep this house together. She had something powerful and important to give, and because she loved her kids and her husband, she wanted to give it. It was not always easy, but the husband and wife have stayed together and have enjoyed many happy years. And their son has achieved more than anyone thought possible.

A little-observed Jewish tradition holds that a couple is supposed to leave a small corner of a room in their home unpainted. As scholars have noted, the practice goes back to a painful time in Jewish history, when the Temple in Jerusa-lem, the central place of worship, had been destroyed. The Jews were distraught, convinced they would never rebuild this holy place. They continued to engage in commerce and study, to celebrate births, marriages, and other special moments, but they resolved to keep one small portion of their homes unfinished as a testament to what had been lost, and as a reminder of what they one day hoped to rebuild.

I like this interpretation of the tradition, but I have a slightly different one. To me, the unpainted corner stands as a reminder of any project that will never be finished. It is always there to be worked on. And that is how healthy, lasting relationships are. They are never finished, never complete; there is always work to be done. There is always more to give.

Today, I integrate that insight into every wedding I perform. Before I marry a couple, we meet in my office so that I can go over the rituals and their meaning. I walk the couple through what is going to happen, allay any fears, and answer any questions. When we discuss the ritual breaking of a glass that concludes all Jewish weddings, I ask the couple if they know what it symbolizes. Isn't it strange that we end such a happy occasion with an act of destruction? Many brides and grooms with Jewish educations will tell me that the act recalls the destruction of the Jewish Temple in Jerusalem and their own inclusion in a community bent on rebuilding. True, I say, but there is another interpretation gleaned from my own life experience of love, relationships, and marriage. The breaking of a glass symbolizes the love between a couple, which is inherently fragile. Take care of your love. Protect it. Give of yourself, so that you may keep your bond strong and vibrant.

Gratitude

∞

Surviving is one thing, thriving quite another. Is it possible to find a new wholeness even as we fully confront the pain of our pasts? Can we discover deep contentment and happiness even amidst illness, grief, family tensions, divorce, economic setbacks, and injustice?

We can't go back to our old lives, and yes, some of our old dreams will almost certainly be lost to us. But by learning to redefine key dimensions of our lives, by learning to see the familiar in new ways, we can gradually gain access to new treasures, discovering richness and meaning where before there seemed none. By shifting our awareness, we can come to enjoy new, deeper pleasures and dream new, deeper dreams.

Over the years of Eyal's illness, many people tried to comfort us by suggesting, with the best of intentions, that we celebrate the wisdom that comes through struggle and heartbreak—that we look for the "silver lining" and regard it as a "hidden blessing" or even "redemption." To me, a new way of seeing and being was small compensation for the anguish and confusion I was experiencing. I didn't want wisdom; I wanted a healthy kid! I would have traded all Solomon's wisdom to have Eyal fully healed.

With time, I have indeed become grateful for the cognitive shifts and resiliency that have allowed me to find a new normal. It is good to know that contentment and happiness are possible, if only we put our minds and hearts to the task of finding it. You can be hurting and still grateful; they are not mutually exclusive.

Experiencing gratitude is itself a pathway to wholeness. In my forty years as a rabbi, counseling those who are hurting, I have witnessed the power of gratitude time and again. If a person can move to a place of giving thanks, all kinds of sadness begin to melt away. Gratitude allows us to become aware of what we have *right now*. We become conscious of presence, not absence. The present moment seems brighter, fuller. We are that much closer to the Promised Land.

Several years ago, I invited a man to speak at a midnight service held at our synagogue the Saturday night before the Jewish New Year. Eyal was in college, and his physical condition was stable, which is to say, he had not been in the hospital for a couple of months. My guest was well known in Jewish circles, a highly respected professor at a prominent university. I invited him not because of his impressive résumé, but because I had read a book he wrote recounting the loss of his young, married daughter, and I had found his writing raw, honest, insightful, and comforting.

I was looking forward to meeting this man and spending time with him one-on-one; maybe I would pick up ideas or strategies to help us as a family. Before the religious service began, we chatted in my office. Clearly he had done his homework, for he turned to me and said, "Chuck, tell me about your son."

I pointed to a large family photograph on the wall, taken at the New York State Fair, before Eyal got sick. Then I showed him a more recent photograph of Eyal in his high school graduation cap and gown, with the honor society sash around his shoulders. My guest spent a few moments in silence looking at the photographs. Then he turned to me. "How do you deal with the pain? Has your faith been shaken?" I did not say much in response to these questions; instead, I just told him the basics of our story. I do remember saying to him, "Life is pretty good."

A few days later, I received a thank-you note from him. Part of it struck me as strange. "Chuck, I can't help but observe that when I asked you to tell me about your son, your answer was odd. The story of your son is obviously compelling, but you tell it with virtually no affect. And when you tell the story, it ends up sounding too much like a recorded announcement. I know you must hurt and hurt a lot. It's okay to let a bit of that out."

I took seriously this claim that I lacked emotion about Eyal, that I was repressing something. But after careful thought, I decided it wasn't true. My guest had expected me to break down in tears while talking about Eyal. Quite possibly, that's because he was unable to tell his daughter's story without feeling strong emotion. I was telling Eyal's story from a different place—a place of peace. And what had brought me there can be summed up in a single word: gratitude. I am thankful for what I have. Today, constantly proclaiming my thankfulness makes me feel even more at peace, content, and able to say without reservation, "Life is pretty good."

• • •

Here's a partial list of big-picture things I feel grateful for: I have Eyal. I'm married to my soul mate. I have four other good kids who like each other. I have my health. I have my faith. I have work and responsibilities I enjoy. I have a nice home. I have close friends on whom I can rely. I have a sense of self-worth and purpose. I have a sense of humor. I have the respect of others in my community.

When people come to me lost and dispirited, questioning their self-worth, I listen carefully without being judgmental. Sometimes I ask them to make a series of lists. Take a legal pad, I tell them, and draw a line down the middle. On one side, write down all of the bad things that have happened. On the other, write down all of the *good* things. On one side, write down what you can't do anymore. On the other side, write down what you *can* do. On one side, list people who have let you down. On the other side, list people who have stood by you.

Inevitably, one list is much longer than the other. And I've never seen the longer one be the list of what's lacking.

Bad things do happen to all of us. But when we're in pain, we tend to focus all our energies on the painful situation, the losses. Making lists like this, we force ourselves to look beyond our pain, to see the whole scope of our lives, and to acknowledge the bigger picture for which we feel grateful.

Gratitude opens our eyes to what we have and the possibilities in front of us. It leads us to discover the previously undiscovered. Consider again the Biblical story of Hagar, the concubine wife of the patriarch Abraham. Hagar does not get along with Sarah, Abraham's wife and true love. At Sarah's instigation, Abraham banishes Hagar and the son she bore him, Ishmael, from their house. Hagar wanders through the wilderness, hungry, thirsty, and alone except for her son. Convinced that he is going to die of thirst, she puts him under a bush to protect him and stands some distance away, not wishing to see him draw his final breath.

Something amazing happens. At precisely the moment when everything appears lost, when Hagar is in tears and convinced her world is coming apart, an angel of God calls to her from the heavens and says, "God has heard the cry of the boy." As the Biblical text states, God then opens Hagar's eyes and she sees a well of water. Filling a skin with it, she lets her boy drink, saving his life.

Many commentators have taken this intervention as a Divine miracle. I like another interpretation. The well was always there, but Hagar had been so consumed with her own fear that she had failed to take notice. Had she managed to break through her fear a bit earlier, she might have seen the well earlier and embarked much sooner on her journey to healing and renewal. It took someone else—in this case, an angel of God—to say, "Hagar, look up, it's right in front of you!"

Negative emotions are extremely seductive, making us feel like we are victims. They can smother us, preventing all healing. Most of us don't have angels of God tapping us on the shoulder and pointing the way, but that's okay; gratitude can serve as that angelic voice, pulling us out of our current misery. By directing our minds to feeling thankful, we allow ourselves to see reality in a startlingly new way, finding solutions in our everyday lives that have been there all along.

Gratitude doesn't always come naturally or easily. Religions have ceremonies and liturgy built into them that lead us to experience feelings of thankfulness, even and especially at the hardest of times.

The Mourner's Kaddish is a core prayer in Judaism, recited every evening, morning, and afternoon for eleven months after the death of a loved one, as well as on the anniversary of the death. Surprisingly, the prayer contains not a single mention of death. What it does say is this: "May God's great name be exalted and hallowed throughout the created world. May God's great name be acknowledged forever and ever! May the name of the Holy One be acknowledged and celebrated, lauded and worshipped, exalted and honored."

The Kaddish contains a litany of adjectives that praise God: "glorified and celebrated," "lauded and praised," "acclaimed and honored," "extolled and exalted." Just imagine, here is a family who has suffered a terrible loss, and yet they are required to praise and thank God. It has to be the farthest thing from their minds! But that's precisely why such a prayer is important. In uttering words of thanks, we're making ourselves more aware of what we have to feel grateful for.

It's easy to feel grateful and retain faith in God when things are running smoothly. But at the hardest of times, the Kaddish prayer takes you by the collar, in the midst of your anguish, and says, *Hey, listen. I know you didn't sign up for this. I know it hurts. But you still have the capacity to appreciate the good in your life. Don't give in to cynicism and despair.*

Most of us will experience cynicism and despair for a while after something bad happens. Just saying a prayer won't prevent it. But over time, and with constant repetition, our hearts just may catch up to our lips. We gain a larger perspective, realizing that there's life beyond the pain we feel. We don't know what tomorrow holds, but we do have today.

A woman whom I have known for thirty-five years was

saying Kaddish for her mother, who had recently passed away. Her elderly parents had moved to Syracuse from New Jersey a couple years earlier, recognizing that they needed help. Her father had been sick, frequently uncommunicative and immobile, and while her mother was alive, she had devoted almost every waking hour to taking care of him. Now that her mother was gone, the grieving daughter was overwhelmed—trying to mourn her mother, with whom she had been very close, but worried all the time about her frail father. If someone did not feed him, he would not eat. If someone did not hold a cup to give him water, he would not drink. She also had her own family to care for, including an adult son with special needs, as well as an important, demanding job. I found myself worrying that there were not enough hours in the day for her. She was drained.

After the death of her mother, this woman came to synagogue early each morning to say the Kaddish. Her anguish and stress were unmistakable, but still she uttered the prayer. After services, I asked how her father was doing. And I said to her, "Be thankful for those moments you *do* have." One morning, after several weeks, I noticed that she had more bounce in her step. She smiled and was more animated. After services, on the way out, I asked my usual question, "How is your father? Was he any better yesterday?"

She reached into her pocketbook for her iPhone and said, "I want you to see something." She showed me a video of her father sitting in a chair in his nursing home, eating an ice cream cone on his own. "I don't know what's happening," this woman said. "He seemed to recognize me. It looked like he was ready to stand up and walk." I said to her, once again, what I had said so many times before: "Be thankful for those moments you *do* have."

This woman had been reeling from the loss of her mother and the painful realization that her father was not going to recover. It was hard for her to feel grateful, as she had been focusing only on her losses. Perhaps the morning routine, the meditative prayer, and a community of like-minded people who were also "walking through the valley" had helped her. Somehow she had managed to let go of her focus on what she wanted—her father's complete recovery—and had come to see what she *did* have. In the midst of her pain, she was able to find something to be excited about. And she felt grateful. Everything wasn't suddenly okay for her, but gratitude offered her at least a measure of contentment.

"Dayeinu" is a song familiar to most people in my faith tradition. We sing it during the Passover Seder. It has a terrific melody and is upbeat, toe-tapping, hand-clapping. It is one of the first songs a Jewish child learns, and yet the content is serious and thoughtful. "Dayeinu" means, "It would have been enough." The song recounts the daily miracles that the children of Israel were exposed to: the splitting of the Red Sea; the gift of the Ten Commandments on Mount Sinai; the appearance of manna, a heavenly food; sweet water springing from a rock. Human nature being what it is, I can imagine them waking up each day feeling entitled to whatever new miracle awaited. When we sing the song, we list each miracle and then repeat "*dayeinu*"—"it should have been enough." The splitting of the sea, *dayeinu*. Mount Sinai, *dayeinu*. Manna, *dayeinu*. "Dayeinu" is a reminder that we must recognize the good things we already have in our lives. It demonstrates a mature understanding of expectation and gratitude. You can still hope for a miracle, you can still yearn for what you do not have, but at all times you must express gratitude for what you have already been given.

I've suggested that to remain optimistic, it's best to start small and relish the little victories we experience in everyday life. This approach is important when it comes to gratitude, too.

You can tell people over and over, "You have so much to be thankful for," but until they come to that point of understanding themselves, it does no good. Sometimes it takes baby steps. To move ahead, we need to discover as many opportunities as possible to feel grateful. We even need to *discipline* ourselves to focus on the good, much as we discipline ourselves to stay present-focused in order to persevere. If we strive to make gratitude a part of our daily lives, we may enjoy the kind of epiphany moments Hagar experiences—again and again. And over time, we may recover a sense of life's majesty and wonder, even despite what we have lost.

Judaism has embedded in it a whole system for nurturing gratitude, above and beyond the Kaddish prayer. Jews are required to recite a minimum of one hundred blessings daily expressing thankfulness. When we awake in the morning, we say a blessing, Modeh Ani, thanking God for restoring our souls to us. It does not get more basic than that. When we go to bed at night, we actually die. And so every time we wake up, it is a gift to be cherished and an opportunity to offer thanksgiving.

As the day progresses, Jews are expected to offer blessings at many other points: upon hearing thunder, upon seeing a rainbow, upon seeing trees blossom for the first time in the year, upon wearing new clothes, upon putting your clothes on, upon physically stretching, upon using something new for the first time, upon eating a piece of bread. These blessings fall into two categories: expressions of gratitude for unusual or new experiences, and expressions of gratitude for the ordinary and mundane. The point is that by acknowledging and expressing appreciation for *all* of it, we come to see everything as special, even the mundane.

Every day, 365 days a year, make a practice of searching out one hundred things to feel thankful for. Don't worry about sticking to one hundred—the exact number isn't important. And don't feel you need to anticipate every occasion for gratitude. Just keeping our eyes open and staying in the moment as blessings present themselves is a great start. Maybe it's a challenge we have enjoyed at work that sparks thankfulness. Or maybe it's hearing a child's giggle. Putting on a warm coat. Receiving a phone call from a friend. Having a spouse or significant other who listens. Sitting through a doctor's exam for something that turns out to be normal. Maybe it's a chance to travel someplace you've never been. Maybe it's a new friendship. A great book. A movie that makes you laugh out loud.

Living in the snow belt as I do, I express thankfulness for a clear, sunny day. I feel gratitude when I come downstairs in the morning and hear that Eyal is doing well. Or when I go to my bagel shop and read the *New York Post* while enjoying a medium French vanilla coffee and poppy-seed bagel. Or when the house quiets down late at night and I sit in my recliner, a few feet away from the television set, remote in hand, channel surfing, with no one else voicing his or her opinion on what we should watch.

It's helpful to pick a specific number of "gratitude moments" each day to shoot for, because it helps us to widen our horizon. And at the end of a long day, when we're eight blessings short of the required one hundred, we embark on a process of discovery and awareness. What do we do? Where do we find those remaining eight blessings to satisfy the law? This process encourages us to think about things we may have taken for granted and recognize them as blessings to add to the count. A shooting star—there's a blessing. The delicious apple in the refrigerator—there's another blessing. A glass of cold water, another blessing. Everything can serve as the occasion for a blessing: the food we eat, the words we say, the actions we take, the clothing we wear, the weather we experience, the people we meet.

The great thing about gratitude is that it's cumulative. A lifetime of this discipline has conditioned me to feel grateful during the hard times I've experienced. During my child-hood, my parents modeled gratitude for me according to Jewish tradition. Every Friday night, I saw my mother say a blessing over candles. We said the blessing over wine and bread. I saw my father pray every morning, uttering words of thanksgiving. After dinner, we said grace. All this left a mark. Although I came from a lower-middle-class family, I felt like I had been given a lot. Gratitude was woven into the fabric of my life. What a wonderful gift to bestow on our children—the capacity for gratitude, the idea that nothing should be taken for granted. When Eyal got sick, my main challenge was to sustain the practice of giving thanks, not discover it for the first time.

I once read about a woman in my community who had lost her daughter in a car accident. A devout Christian, she grieved for her daughter and felt abandoned by God, to the point that she gave up her usual evening prayers. Miss-ing the sense of peace her prayers had given her, she willed herself to thank God for just one thing that had happened each day. Slowly, painfully, she continued the practice. Over time, she came to thank God for two or three things that had happened in a day. That was her road to gratitude, and ultimately, to healing.

The Onondaga War Memorial is a large, unattractive, barn-like building that serves as our local venue for minor-league ice hockey, class B professional wrestling, high school basketball games, the circus, *Disney on Ice*, and in mid-June, ten or twelve local high school graduations. On June 24, 1998, we, the Shermans of Syracuse, took our seats as Eyal received his diploma from Nottingham High School.

Eyal sat on the auditorium floor with four hundred of his fellow classmates. Leah sat next to him, along with his nurse and teacher's aide. Several minutes before his name was called, Leah maneuvered his motorized wheelchair onto an automatic lift that would transport him to stage level for the presentation. When his name was called, he used a switch on his wheelchair, activated by a subtle motion of his chin, to move across the stage with Leah not far behind to collect his diploma.

I watched from the bleachers, as did everybody else. I couldn't believe we had reached this moment. It was an act of defiance and of affirmation. All those doubters who told us he would never reach this day were proven wrong.

Upon seeing Eyal's wheelchair, everybody in this huge auditorium fell into silence. Then his fellow classmates rose to their feet and began applauding. This surprised me. Nottingham is a tough school; only about half the students who enter ninth grade graduate, and many of Eyal's classmates didn't engage with the world or profess to care about very much. Yet row after row of them rose up, joined by their friends and family members, until soon everyone in the six-thousand-seat arena was standing. The applause grew and grew, minute after minute.

My lips quivered. Tears rolled down my cheeks, I turned to the side so my other children wouldn't see me cry.

Usually when we think of parents attending graduations, we think of them beaming with pride. While I was proud of Eyal and all he had accomplished, what I felt more than anything else was gratitude.

There is a blessing called a Shehecheyanu that Jews recite at rites of passage—a baby naming, a Bar or Bat Mitzvah, a wedding, just about any happy occasion. But the blessing is not reserved for those big events. Jews can say it at any time to recognize those moments when gratitude washes over us. Watching Eyal that day, I said the Shehecheyanu to myself.

Thank you for granting us life, for sustaining us, and for helping us to reach this day.

Joy

∞

In the spring of 1987, when Eyal was still living in that cramped Syracuse hospital room, his prognosis grim, our oldest child, Nogah, turned thirteen. She was looking more and more like Leah: tall, slim, long brown hair, red highlights, bangs touching her eyebrows. She was at the awkward glasses-and-braces stage—not quite a woman, but not a little girl. Her Bat Mitzvah was coming up soon, a much-anticipated event. Nogah loved synagogue life, relishing the special attention that came with being the rabbi's kid. She ran around the building, knew all the hiding places, ascended the pulpit, sat next to me at the end of services. She was well prepared for her Bat Mitzvah; growing up in a rabbinic family, she had picked up a lot through osmosis and had heard dozens of kids chant the blessings and deliver their speeches at their Bar and Bat Mitzvahs. She knew what to expect and was excited.

One early April Saturday afternoon, a few weeks before the big day, Nogah and I chatted about her Bat Mitzvah as we walked home from synagogue. Another Bar Mitzvah had taken place that morning with a large, sumptuous buffet luncheon. A big party, with a band, dancing, and a festive dinner, would take place that night. The party's theme would be Syracuse University basketball, complete with basketball centerpieces and orange balloons, and a half court with a freestanding basket at the ballroom's entrance.

As usual, I offered a little critique on the Bar Mitzvah during our walk home. "I thought he did really well today. He seemed more relaxed than I did." When I asked Nogah what she thought, she replied simply, "It was good."

We had walked about halfway down the hill between the synagogue and our house and Nogah, head down, was kicking a stone. "Nogah, it looks like it's going to be a fun party tonight."

She kept kicking the stone. "Yeah."

"The Steinbergs will pick you up around seven thirty. I'm going to be at the hospital with Ema. I'll try to stop in later on. Wish them a mazel tov. But I need you to try and get a ride home with somebody."

"Okay." A few moments of silence followed, which was unnatural for Nogah, who was usually bubbly and talkative.

"Nogah, is anything wrong?"

"No."

More silence. I tried again. "Nogah, there's something bothering you. What's wrong?"

She stopped and turned to me. "Abba, I'm afraid to tell you. I don't want to hurt you and Ema."

"Nogah, please stop. You can tell me."

Her lower lip quivered and tears filled her eyes. "Abba, I don't want a Bat Mitzvah if Eyal can't be there."

I understood what Nogah was feeling. I felt the same way. For years before Eyal got sick, I had been looking forward to Nogah's Bat Mitzvah. Our out-of-town family—a large contingent—would travel to Syracuse to attend, and they would see me on my home turf for the first time. I was thrilled to show off my synagogue and my rabbinic skills. Leah and I had talked—back when life was easier for us—about the kind of party we would throw: a festive Friday evening Shabbat dinner, a big luncheon on Saturday, a party at night, a brunch the next morning. We wanted to raise the bar. Nogah was the rabbi's daughter.

But she was right. Picking up on my own ambivalence, she had identified the issue that had been bubbling under the surface. I, too, did not have my heart in her Bat Mitzvah. I wasn't talking much about it. I had procrastinated on the planning, and with only a couple of weeks left, I hadn't yet spoken to a florist or finalized the menus. I felt guilt. Pain. Fatigue. Most of all, I asked myself: How can we celebrate without Eyal? How can we celebrate a happy occasion with our hearts so heavy?

When children ask us difficult questions, it's not like we can say, "Let me think about that awhile, and I'll get back to you." We have to answer in the moment, doing the best that we can. And I had to respond to Nogah as honestly as possible. I had to give her an answer that would satisfy not just her, but me as well.

We moved into a driveway, out of the way of oncoming cars. I hugged her. She held on tight. We stood there a moment while I collected my thoughts. "Nogah," I said, "I understand more than you think. I'm sorry. Ema and I are so proud of you. Of course you're going to have your Bat Mitzvah. Even though Eyal is not going to be there, he *is* going to be there; we know that. Friday night after dinner, we'll go and see him. Saturday afternoon, we'll do the same. Aunt Lil has asked to be with him when we can't be at the hospital. She gives great back rubs and tickles and loves to tell him stories. Eyal won't be alone the whole weekend. We'll all be sad Eyal won't be with us, but we'll also be happy. Sometimes in life you're a little sad, but you can be happy, too."

My life until Eyal got sick was pretty good. I never gave much thought to joy and happiness, for they came as naturally to me as breathing. We were blessed. Leah and I loved being the parents of a large, young, active family. Our kids had all four of their grandparents alive and in good health. As a rabbi, when I interacted with people whose lives were in turmoil, I felt sad and tried to offer comfort and encouragement, but I didn't understand firsthand what they were going through. It was easy and somewhat patronizing for me to say, "Well, life goes on." At the end of the day, it was not my loss.

And yet, life *does* go on. We tend to look at people who have experienced some kind of disaster and think they must be absolutely miserable. How could they possibly know joy again? Haven't we all seen people who have lost a loved one and never recovered? But the older we get, the more all of us experience losses. A loved one dies. A relationship ends. We lose a physical or mental capacity through illness or aging. We are fired from a job. We think we will never get over these things—that life might as well end for us—but we do. We heal. We regenerate. We move on. We laugh again. We live again. We forget the pain, only to have it return, like an old throbbing wound, when some event in the present reminds us of it. Each of us has a tremendous capacity to recover from hurt and still retain it. Rebuilding our lives requires us to do both.

In the early years of Eyal's illness, I found it hard to experience joy. I did not want to go to wedding receptions, birthday parties, wedding anniversary celebrations. I just didn't feel like going onto the dance floor and dancing to "Hava Nagillah." If I was in this kind of pain, I thought, how could everybody else go on and laugh, sing, and celebrate? When someone told a funny joke, I wanted to laugh, but I held it in. Having delivered hundreds of eulogies, I knew that jokes offered a welcome relief. But when it came to my own pain, I did not want to laugh.

Nogah's Bat Mitzvah was both a milestone and a test. With Leah's help, I rose to the challenge. We met with the caterer and selected a menu befitting a queen. We ordered light-blue yarmulkes with a personalized keepsake mono-gram. We let Nogah choose any cake she wanted and allowed her to invite her summer camp friends to stay at our house for the weekend. The day of the Bat Mitzvah, Nogah felt con-fident and happy. As promised, throughout the weekend, Eyal enjoyed a continuous stream of visitors. Saturday night, we had the party at home. We sang, danced, laughed, and celebrated. We successfully navigated the difficult intersec-tion of pain and joy.

Sometimes the intersection of pain and joy is a literal one. In the United States, drivers respect the funeral cortege trav-eling on its way to the cemetery. Cars pull to the side with proper care and diligence. Traffic laws allow the hearse to go through red lights and stop signs. In Judaism, we regard such practices as consistent with our concept of *kavod hamet*— respect for the dead. Judaism also demonstrates such respect through preparations and rituals. For example, the deceased is never left unattended; a *shomer,* a guard, recites psalms beside the coffin. Judaism likewise accords weddings—a paramount experience of joy—a similar level of respect. It is customary to offer public blessings and good wishes to the betrothed prior to the marriage, and in some congregations to shower the groom with candy thrown from the pews. This likely reflects excitement about what a wedding represents: sacred intimacy, creation, newness, the anticipation of a sweet life for the newlyweds.

Rabbinic literature poses an intriguing question: What happens if a funeral cortege and a wedding processional arrive at the same time at the same intersection? Which has the right of way? In the United States, the answer is simple: the wedding procession waits as the funeral cortege continues on its journey. In Jewish tradition, it is the opposite. The funeral cortege waits, and the wedding procession rolls on. The point here isn't about traffic patterns and traffic control. Jewish tradition embodies a philosophy of life. At that intersection of joy/happiness and sadness/pain, joy and happiness take precedence, even when we possess a heavy heart and a broken spirit.

When Nogah told me she didn't want a Bat Mitzvah because Eyal couldn't be there, she was saying, "I am uncomfortable being so happy with Eyal so sick." She needed me to tell her, "It's all right, even under these circumstances, to celebrate." And more important than my telling her, she needed me to set the example by being joyful myself. The statement I was making by enjoying myself on her big day was, "You can't feel guilty during life's happy moments. You feel the absence of a loved one perhaps, you once in a while say, 'Boy, I wish he was here,' but in the end, joy trumps sorrow."

We sometimes have a strange kind of loyalty to our sense of loss. We feel guilty about having a good time again. We think that by laughing and celebrating, we are abandoning past relationships. We think in terms of either/or—you experience either joy or sadness, but not both. In the Book of Ecclesiastes, we discover the oft-quoted verses "For everything there is a season . . . A time to cast away stones, and a time to gather stones together, a time to weep and a time to laugh." In real life, it's not so simple. No divide evenly separates happy and sad times. They often come intermingled. During life's sad times, joyful moments arise, even if it's a few seconds of laughter. We have to reach out, grasp that joy, and hold on as long as we can.

Each fall, Jews celebrate the holiday of Sukkot, commemorating the Israelites' forty years of wandering in the desert by eating outdoors in temporary huts. The experience helps Jews relive the tenuousness of the Israelites' journey, their vulnerability to the weather and to the many dangers encountered during their nomadic wanderings. However, the Biblical mandate that frames the Sukkot festival is not about reassurance and encouragement but rather something different: "You shall be joyful." How can we legislate joy? How can we tell someone who is unhappy to be happy? How can we tell someone who is terrified to celebrate? That Biblical mandate implies an understanding that joy does not always come naturally. We have to *work* at it. Sometimes we almost have to will ourselves to be joyful.

During our years in hospitals, we often found patients and their families making a point of inserting joy into otherwise grim circumstances. On one memorable occasion, a child with an aggressive brain lesion was turning five. Despite his infirmity, the staff and relatives of a number of other sick kids made a huge party, decorating the floor's playroom with balloons, cartoon-character tablecloths, and silly party hats. For an hour or so, all the kids ran around, played, ate cake and ice cream, and had a great time. One girl, six-year-old Emily, her body skeletal and her head bald and shiny because of treatment for a catastrophic blood disorder, wore a fresh unsoiled hospital gown, attractive ruby nail polish on her little toes and fingers, and the crowning glory, a reminder of her femininity, a multicolored ribbon on her head. She and her parents, with the angel of death hovering, joyfully shouted, "Happy birthday," celebrating and affirming life.

We can't wait for joy to come to us. When a child is sick and does not want to eat, what does the parent say? "You have to have some juice. You have to have some soup. It will make you feel better." Likewise, we have to create an environment that welcomes joy in, little by little. A recent widow might make a lunch date with an old friend; a person whose marriage has fallen apart might put the pain on the shelf for an afternoon to play tennis; a family caregiver may take a day trip to enjoy a change of scenery.

After Nogah's Bat Mitzvah, I forced myself to be social and have fun—to stop by that party, go to that basketball game, even if just for a couple of minutes. I didn't want to become stuck in life and defined by my suffering and pain; I wouldn't be good company for other people and certainly not for myself. I was learning that even my best friends would listen to my lamentations for a time, but that nobody wanted to be around somebody who just wallowed endlessly in misery. That made sense, since wallowing was counterproductive. It didn't get me anywhere.

I have since welcomed joy into my life without reservation. Thanks to my job, I'm exposed more than most to some pretty happy moments. It does not get any better than officiating at the wedding of young people whose naming ceremonies I presided over years ago, or better yet, conducting the naming ceremonies for their own children when they have them. I don't feel guilty anymore about celebrating, smiling, laughing. It's not that I deny my pain, but I experience a freedom, a feeling of release, when I let it go and simply enjoy the moment.

For years, despite whatever challenges Leah and I were experiencing, we have made a point of going out for dinner three or four nights a week, sometimes with the kids, sometimes on our own. This was our little slice of time, a chance to reconnect, and to the extent we could, to enjoy. We must also allow ourselves to find joy in places and experiences we previously ignored or overlooked or misunderstood. My oldest grandson, Yehuda, is now four years old, the age Eyal was when he took sick. I long imagined I would feel torn watching my grandchildren swing on the swing set or slide down a slide, remembering when Eyal could do those things. But I have been able to play joyfully with Yehuda, to tickle him, chase after him in the yard, play catch with him, watch him dig in the sand, without that sadness tugging at me. When we are tested, we discover joy in places we never before imagined.

In Deuteronomy, the last of the Five Books of Moses, Moses has reached the end of his road and is about to die. Yet even here, his farewell message to a people that has both inspired him and challenged him is *"Uvarchata b'chayim"*: "Choose life."

Sometimes we can arrive at a place where we find joy even in the thing that caused us pain. One day after Eyal had started to attend public school, we were surprised when he returned one afternoon almost in tears. Apparently, the social studies classroom was a zoo, with the kids misbehaving and talking out of turn. The teacher, in an act of desperation, had decided on a punitive homework assignment: everyone had to write, one hundred times, "I promise not to talk during class." Because Eyal writes by using a mouth stick to access his computer, this assignment would have taken a long time. But it was not the length of the assignment that troubled him. "It sucks," he told us. "It's not fair. Even if I wanted to talk out loud in class, she knows I can't. Why should I do this stupid assignment?"

Leah and I looked at each other, trying to act like the grown-ups in the room but at the same time trying to conceal our amusement and silence our giggles. If one of the other kids had come home with this punishment, and we found out that he or she had been disruptive, we would have been furious. We have tried to teach our kids respect for authority figures, in particular teachers. But this was Eyal. It was nice to know that we had reached a point where others could see him not as the kid with special needs, but as just another one of the fifth graders at Ed Smith Elementary School who needed to be reminded about appropriate classroom behavior. It was a small moment, but a joyful one.

To survive the kind of pain we've struggled with over a long period, we have had to create a culture of joy. Most folks think that because of my rabbinic calling and the fact that my son is so sick, our house must be a somber place. Not so! In the early days, I would get everybody together and hold a Sunday-afternoon "showtime." We probably performed every popular Disney story. My favorite was *Cinderella*, with me as Prince Charming in my tuxedo; Eyal's nurse recruited to be the Fairy Godmother; Nogah playing Cinderella; Orah playing a stepsister; Leah serving as the director and costume designer; the boys, Erez and Eyal, acting as the royal coachmen (picture both wearing mouse ears and charcoal mouse whiskers, with Eyal in his wheelchair); and Nitza, our youngest, as an audience of one.

The kids picked up on my silliness, my attempt to lighten the mood, and my reassurance that it was all right to be happy and to laugh. On a number of occasions, Orah put on water shows with her store-bought, synthetic-rubber, twelve-inch killer whale Shamu and a hospital basin. Nogah took latex medical gloves and filled them with water, making water balloons. Even Eyal laughed and smiled, and thank goodness for that. It would have been an extra burden for Eyal to think that his illness was making everyone in the family sad.

My parents passed away in 2007, when Eyal was a sophomore in college. My mother died first, buried in Philadelphia. A few months later, my father died and was buried next to my mother. After my father's service, I stood at the graveside next to several elderly aunts and cousins. I admit I hadn't been good about keeping in touch. We hugged and embraced. "Chuckie, let's get together for happy times, too," they said to me. I had heard those words so many times over the years, in places like this. But this time, the words truly resonated.

About a year later, on Valentine's Day, a Sunday evening, we celebrated Nogah's wedding at Har Zion Temple in Philadelphia, where she was a rabbi and director of education. Leah had grown up at this synagogue, and we had been married there thirty-eight years earlier. When Nogah got engaged, I told myself that her wedding would take place in Philadelphia. All of my relatives were older; they lived in

Philadelphia, and they wouldn't be able to travel to Syracuse. I wanted my family present. And I remembered those words, "Chuckie, let's get together for happy times, too." Taking into consideration Eyal's needs, it would have been easier financially to marry Nogah on my pulpit in Syracuse. If we had the wedding in another city, we would have to hire nurses to travel with us and transport all of Eyal's medical equipment, supplies, and even a hospital bed for the hotel. But I wanted to do it. I had replayed that conversation in my head over and over: "Let's get together for happy times."

I had the honor of officiating at the wedding with the help of our younger son, Erez, himself a rabbi in California. I also enjoyed the privilege of escorting Nogah down the aisle with Leah. I ascended the steps of the pulpit, arm in arm with Leah. Then, in line with Jewish tradition, Nogah circled Scott, the groom, as I looked out onto the congregation. Leah was to my left, while Orah and Nitza served as attendants. Erez stood next to Eyal, whom he had wheeled down the aisle several moments earlier. Eyal sat erect, wearing a tuxedo, a shirt with studs and French cuffs, and a black bow tie, his sandy brown hair groomed meticulously.

Before we chanted the ceremony's blessings, Nogah and I made eye contact. She was at the same time anxious and excited. Tears of joy fell down her cheeks. I reached out for her hand across the table that held the sacramental wine, as well as a glass to be broken at the end of the wedding. I thought about the conversation we had had all those years ago, when she said to me, "Abba, I don't want a Bat Mitzvah if Eyal can't be there." I thought about the answer I had given her, that it was all right, even in the midst of pain, to celebrate. That sometimes in your life you're a little sad, but you can be happy, too.

Epilogue

∞

I was a young father when Eyal first got sick, when all this began. Now I am a grandfather and nearing retirement. Looking back, I realize that what happened to Eyal had the potential to destroy our family. Eyal's siblings could have easily grown up angry, resenting the time and energy that Eyal required during their childhoods. They could have rejected our belief system, our traditions, our robust faith. If they had, I would have understood. But our family stayed happy and intact. Nogah and Erez joined "the family business" and became rabbis. Orah became director of student life at the Jewish Theological Seminary of America, the same school we all graduated from. Each married and now has children of his or her own. Nitza, the baby Leah was carrying when Eyal first became ill, is a nurse, providing care to kids with many of the same problems Eyal has.

Leah is still Leah: a woman of indomitable strength and courage who has taught us all that sometimes you just have to suck it up and do whatever is necessary. She has devoted her life to caring for Eyal and at the same time has been a remarkable wife, lover, daughter, and mother. Out of extraordinary difficulties, circumstances that would bring most of us to our knees, she has managed to craft a relatively normal life. In Leah's world, there is no time for pity, regret, or second-guessing. No patience for it, either.

It took me a long time to find myself. Once we accept we are not the same person we thought we were, we start down the road to healing and recovery. I have learned I can live happily, responsibly, and joyfully—that I can love others—even though I sometimes have a broken heart.

I have learned that it's all right to be sad and it's all right as an adult man to cry. I have learned the importance of community and the warmth of Jewish ritual. I have felt the comfort of being embraced even by those with whom I may have disagreed, be it when I was lifted on a chair at my daughter's wedding or when dirt was tossed on my mother's grave. I learned that many answers I thought I had as a rabbi were not particularly convincing or comforting. I learned the truth about unresolved issues: you learn to live with them, but they are always there. I learned that no shortcuts exist in this highway of life, and all of us at one time or another must walk through "the valley." But I learned that we are all survivors and that the criterion for friendship is just being there. I learned I can still sometimes be really angry at God and yet remain a believer in a sacred relationship.

Life for our family is still tough—and unpredictable. In just the past year, Eyal's eyes have become serious concerns. Because of his compromised brain stem, Eyal doesn't blink normally and runs the risk of corneal breakdowns. Years ago, surgery partially closed his eyes in order to protect his corneas, leaving them open wide enough so that he could see, but this served as only a partial remedy. Now we learned that one of his corneas was on the verge of breakdown; if that happened, he would require major—and dangerous—

transplant surgery. We would have to sew this eye even more tightly closed, changing the way his face looked and compromising a significant part of his vision. This news hit Leah and me hard. Eyal had so little in life, and now he was losing even more. I wondered how Eyal would see himself if his face became deformed—one more piece of his personhood stripped away.

Hard as it is, life goes on. Once again, we used the strategies in this book to start rebuilding—finding another new normal. It's sort of like the story of Moses shattering the Ten Commandments upon returning from Mount Sinai and witnessing the people's disobedience. God's response was clear and straightforward: there's no time for self-pity. Moses climbed the mountain again for a second set of tablets. And the rest is history.

Life for Eyal remains a daily challenge. He still lives at home with Leah and me. We get him out as often as his health permits, allowing him to experience services at the synagogue, window-shopping at local malls, visits to county parks, walks around the neighborhood. Eyal listens to music and watches *Wheel of Fortune* and *Dancing with the Stars*. He follows sports, especially the Syracuse Orange. And he still paints, mostly flowers.

Eyal has had a hard time watching his brother and sisters leave the nest, spread their wings, and pursue their adult lives. But he brightens when they come home to visit. All the kids understand that they must juggle their schedules and professional obligations so that they can all visit home at the same time. Eyal is the magnet that brings everybody back together.

One such visit took place on Labor Day weekend 2012. Everybody returned with their spouses and children, traveling from London, Los Angeles, and Philadelphia. The house was full, every available couch and bed taken, air mattresses set up, toys and sippy cups strewn everywhere. It gave us a feeling of pleasant chaos. Friday night was our Shabbat dinner. As per family tradition, we ate ethnic foods: gefilte fish, hot horseradish, rich yellow braided challah bread, thick sweet Malaga wine, chicken soup with fluffy matzo balls, potato and sweet noodle kugel puddings, roasted chicken, brisket with gravy, kishka (stuffed derma) and rugelach, a pastry. Everyone wore his or her nicest clothing. The meal took place at a leisurely pace. Leah brought out the best china, the hand-embroidered tablecloth, the sterling. We placed the candles in our family heirloom candelabra on the table.

This night, as always, the Shabbat meal began with the Kiddush, a long prayer in Hebrew sung over a cup of wine celebrating Shabbat and creation. We called upon Eyal to say the Kiddush with his younger brother, Erez. We have always done this; it was our way of giving Eyal a role, helping him feel included, even though he couldn't eat the delicious food or participate in other ways. Eyal picked up the Kiddush melody on his own, from years of sitting at the Shabbat table.

When Eyal sings, his mouth opens wide but no sound comes out. Still, in his own way he really does belt out the words. And this evening was no exception. "Eyal, it's your turn now. Loud and slow," I reminded him. As everybody's eyes turned toward him, Nogah, his oldest sibling, said, "Eyal, remember, real loud." And he began, with the rest of us joining him at the appropriate places with spirited singing.

Although Eyal cannot eat, we do make exceptions. In Jewish tradition, we cannot make a blessing without following it with some kind of immediate action; a blessing without action is considered worthless and invalid. If you say the blessing over the wine, you'd better drink the wine. Just like the other kids, Eyal has his own Kiddush cup, a gift from us when he was born. Since this evening was Shabbat, we permitted him several small drops of wine to fulfill the commandment. By now, we knew to expect the redness of the wine to ooze around his trache site and trickle onto the protective trache pads. Remembering how much Eyal loved to eat before he took sick, we also went against all medical advice and allowed Eyal his own soup bowl with three or four teaspoons of the traditional Friday-evening soup. Leah made sure the balloon attached to Eyal's trache was fully inflated to prevent any kind of guck going down the wrong tube, getting into his lungs, and causing pneumonia. Almost immediately, she suctioned out the chicken soup that still went down the wrong pipe.

It was a high-energy meal, with multiple conversations going on at once; Leah jumping up and down to get more soda, another fork, another knife; babies being passed from person to person. I took a moment to take it all in. I thought about my parents and how they would have loved this. The little ones, comfortable and at ease with Eyal, climbing onto his wheelchair, touching all the high-tech buttons and switches. They rubbed his arms, squeezed his fingers. Eyal loved the attention.

A verse in the Bible says, "When you have eaten and are satisfied, you shall praise the Lord your God." And so we sang the traditional Grace After Meal liturgy, everybody taking his or her own part according to family tradition. In Hebrew, Eyal sang, "Rebuild Jerusalem the Holy City soon and in our day," and we responded to his prayer with a resounding "Amen."

At first blush, it might appear as if this prayer is about

Jerusalem, the city that everybody always seems to be fighting over. But our "amen" was forceful that night because as we sat around our Shabbat table, we knew it was not about Jerusalem the city, or any city, but Jerusalem as a state of mind. Each of us has his or her own Jerusalem that is presently shattered and broken. Rebuilding Jerusalem is about fully rebuilding dreams, collective and personal; hopes; and opportunities. It is about fully rebuilding faith and belief. It is about envisioning a time when all things that are broken will be fixed—when we will no longer have to carry the broken and the whole together. For us, the Shermans of Syracuse, saying "amen" that night was about a time when our Eyal would once again sit at our Shabbat table, his body no longer infirm, his voice no longer mute. Then our Jerusalem would be rebuilt.

From Eyal

∞

When I was around five years old, I was lying in a bed in a hospital in New York City. My parents brought a wheelchair into my room and asked me if I wanted to sit in it. My mother remembers that I wanted no part of that chair. I was too young to realize the benefits of getting out of bed. If my parents hadn't encouraged me to—or better yet insisted that I—sit in the chair, my life would have been no more interesting than if I were living inside a doorknob. I didn't have a choice. So they lifted me from the bed to the chair.

Once I was in the wheelchair, I was closer to being able to go home. My brother and sisters were so happy when I came home. They walked in the house after school and saw me sitting in the wheelchair in the family room.

Once I was home, I had an important decision to make: *to do or not to do*. I had to decide whether to sit and look at the walls all day or do something with my life. The consequence of doing nothing was that I would be bored. There would be better consequences if I decided to do something. Going places and doing things enriches your life. It expands your horizons. So I decided to go out and do things. This had a snowball effect on me and a lot of other people. It was just like one of my favorite storybooks from when I was little, *If You Give a Mouse a Cookie*, where one thing leads to another.

When I see people doing all kinds of things, it makes me have the urge to do what they are doing, too. What I've learned is *there is more to life than just sitting in a wheelchair.*

> It isn't fair
> I'm in a wheelchair,
> But I can do things that you wouldn't dare
> If you see me rolling by,
> Just give a smile and say Hi!

I have a dream, that someday I will be able to walk and overcome all of my disabilities and God shall answer each and every one of our prayers, and when that day comes, it will truly be a miracle.

LOVE,
EYAL

I once asked Eyal, "Why do you paint flowers?"
He thought for a few moments and said, "Because you have them forever."

Author's Note

This book would not have been possible without the generous support I received from others who believed that Eyal's story needed to be told. My heartfelt thanks go to Kathleen Curtis, my friend, teacher, and sounding board. Seth Schulman, my gifted literary mentor, set the highest standards for me as well as for himself, teaching me the difference between preaching and writing. I am grateful to Lorin Rees, my literary agent, for his unfailing steadfastness, balance, insight, and lack of ego. Whitney Frick, my editor at Scribner, was not intimidated by my rabbinic persona and knew exactly how this book should be written. Her editing was meticulous and she demonstrated great patience with a first-time author. My secretary, Hope Bratt, was always there to make my work at the synagogue easier. As I frequently remind her, every clergy person should have Hope in his life.

Thank you, too, to my synagogue community for their loyalty and understanding. You allowed me to be a father and a husband during incredibly trying times. Most of all, you allowed me to be me.

I wish to acknowledge those extraordinary members of the medical community who saw past Eyal's diagnosis and appreciated his passion for life, his idiosyncrasies, his "Eyal-ness." Thank you to the late Dr. Fred Epstein, Dr. Mark Helfaer, Dr. Ronald Dubowy, Dr. Paul Cohen, and Dr. David Landsberg. To the many caregivers, Eyal's loyal and dedicated nurses in particular, who came into our home and became part of our family circle—we never would have made it without you. Thank you for making us laugh and for sharing our anguish and fears.

To my children Nogah, Orah, Erez, Nitza, David, Scott, and Nicole: your unfailing commitment to Eyal makes me so proud. I am grateful as well to Eyal's aunts and uncles, his many cousins, and my closest friend, Rabbi Seymour Rosenbloom. Although my parents, Edward and Anne Sherman, and Leah's parents, Bertram and Sadie Hurowitz, are no longer with us, I will always hold them close to my heart. They provided loving support and comfort, doing whatever was necessary, for many years.

Thank you, finally, to Eyal. You are probably the closest thing to an angel I will ever meet. You express no bitterness, no acrimony, no meanness, never a sense of "why me." For you, every moment is the best moment of your life. You have taught me the real meaning of the psalmist who said, "This is the day the Lord has made, let us exalt and rejoice in it."